RELIGIOUS ETHICS
A Systems Approach

PRENTICE-HALL INTERNATIONAL INC., *London*
PRENTICE-HALL OF AUSTRALIA, PTY. LTD., *Sydney*
PRENTICE-HALL OF CANADA, LTD. *Toronto*
PRENTICE-HALL OF INDIA PRIVATE LIMITED, *New Delhi*
PRENTICE-HALL OF JAPAN, INC., *Tokyo*

RELIGIOUS ETHICS
A Systems Approach

JAMES F. SMURL

Oklahoma State University

PRENTICE-HALL, INC.
Englewood Cliffs, New Jersey

ISBN: C 0-13-773051-9
ISBN: P 0-13-773044-6

Library of Congress Catalog Card Number: 78-159447

Printed in the United States of America

10   9   8   7   6   5   4   3   2   1

Preface

IN A TIME WHEN STUDIES of religion far outstrip the practice of it, we may profit in approaching religious ethics from some of the new perspectives made possible in our day. Many of us hesitate to come to this subject with a partisan attitude, intent on promoting some particular religious ethic. We prefer a more comprehensive angle dealing with religious ethics as a category embracing a number of particular religions. Furthermore, we do not wish to superimpose one particular form of doing religious ehtics on all examples of it and need to approach them with a viewpoint which might be called the "detached-within."[1] Such an approach can be had by using the tools of contemporary scientific studies in systems and systems analysis. The language and thought patterns in this field are being widely used today, and suggest several possible models for understanding human activities in which there are a number of variables. For example, the identification of some of the constants and patterned relationships in religious ethics can provide a useful tool in dealing with behavior that is religiously inspired, as well as with that which is not so. At a time when many have tired of purely partisan religion, and pedantic philosophies

---

* Data from pp. 1–8 in INTRODUCTION TO RELIGION: A PHENOMENOLOGICAL APPROACH by Winston L. King (New York: Harper & Row, Publishers, 1968).

[1] Five points of view in the study of religion: 1) "from within"—the religiously partisan inside, 2) "from the semi-within"—the insider aware that his tradition has an outer skin seen by others, 3) "from the semi-without"—the believer who becomes a theologian and/or philosopher of *his* religious tradition, 4) "from without"—the fully detached outsider view of the scientist looking *at* religion, and 5) "from the detached-within"—the interpretative art of the student of religion, detached from truth/value judgments of any one in particular, and sympathetically "within" all.

analyzing language, a systems approach can open up fresh insights as to what the "old" really were, and provide challenging vistas for projecting what the "new" might become.

Doing religious ethics is, after all, a human activity, and should not be made to appear mystifying and abstruse. It involves not only the making of statements such as moral principles, but also includes explicit or implicit convictions about man, the world, and history. When religious ethicians construct and revise their models of human behavior, their work can be partially understood by breaking it down into three analyzable components (process, people, and principles). By isolating these key factors and studying their mutual inter-relationships, we can come to terms not only with the work of a particular ethician, but also with the procedure called "the art of religious ethics."

Whether of the east or the west, religious ethicians seem to have a great deal in common when they "do" ethics. We can call these commonalities a procedure, or art, and can view it as something basically human, and imitable by others who may or may not be doing religious ethics. People might well practice this art when they explain marriage, war, or race relations to others, and might do a better job if they possessed the art more consciously and purposefully.

In the pursuit of such a goal, I offer this study in understanding and applying the art of religious ethics. In doing so I gratefully acknowledge that it is the result of a loving wife named Mary, an education in and by the Diocese of Scranton, Pennsylvania, encouragement from Oklahoma State's faculties of Humanities and Religion, and financial support from its Research Foundation, the secretarial help of Patty Harrison, Marsha Forbes, and Nancy Fancy, as well as the insightful criticism of some alert and sensitive students and colleagues who reacted to these materials during the past year.

James F. Smurl
Oklahoma State University

Table
of
Contents

RELIGIOUS ETHICS
A Systems Approach

chapter one

What Happens
In Religious Ethics

RELIGIOUS ETHICS is a sometimes puzzling phenomenon, yet one that cannot be ignored without a loss to the treasury of mankind's insights and skills. Something of the kind has always existed and promises to be with us in the near future. Preliterate peoples had totems and taboos; literate cultures have their customs and codes; reflective thinkers have sought to either defend or demolish the values and norms developed in various religious traditions. Many people still look to religious teachers for guidance on complex behavioral questions such as those concerned with war and marriage, social and political realities, and any number of matters that may be called purely personal. Hence, an understanding of religious ethics is imperative for one who would understand the human experience, and the ways in which men have relied upon religious thinkers for guidance in both the simple and complex matters of daily life.

There is yet another reason for grappling with the art of religious ethics, and that is for the insights it yields with respect to the processes involved in creating and revising religious schemes of behavior. Knowledge of the operations performed by a religious ethician helps us understand not only what the ethician himself was doing, but also suggests models for doing something similar ourselves. Without such understanding we are more easily manipulated. But one who knows the premises and processes which led to the conclusions can utilize ethical schemes much more wisely.

Thus, there are two very good reasons why twentieth-century Americans should be able to come to terms with religious ethics. But there are many good suggestions as to how that is to be accomplished. There have been and still are a number of excellent methods of approaching the phenomena

1

associated with religious ethics, but none are so normative as to be sacred
and inviolable. And none are so totally helpful that they cannot stand some
assistance from newer experimental approaches. We will find, among others,
studies of religious ethics that offer a more or less strictly objective history of
what has happened in one or several traditions of religious values. We may
also find studies done on the basis of some agreed-upon premises (such. as
those written to the believers in some particular tradition), and which then
proceed to spell out the guidelines for behavior that are consistent with these
commonly-held premises. And we will find still others that are critical studies
helping readers develop sharper powers of discernment into the assumptions
behind ethical statements or in the proper application of ethical principles
to the circumstances of life. What is offered here is not intended to replace or
supplant these methods, but rather to supplement and enrich them with a
methodology derived from contemporary thought on the dynamic interrelationships of various factors within operating unities like a religious ethic.
The approach to be taken here will operate on the basic conviction that
some religious teachings which are normally considered in isolation from
each other, namely, those dealing with history, the nature of man, and the
guidelines for human behavior, ought rather to be studied in the light of
their functional interaction. It will assume that religious insight into what is
desirable or valuable tends to get transformed into coherent ethical schemes
and will proceed to demonstrate the systematic inter-relationship of the
various factors in these schemes.

The Art of Religious Ethics

ITS FORMULATION

One of the first questions that comes to a person's mind when he observes
the phenomenon called religious ethics is "how did they manage to come up
with that?" It may be a particular religious teaching on a matter like stealing or a more generic religious perspective like a general construct about
the meaning of all of human life and activity. In either case the question
about the source and origin of such statements is totally in order. Hence,
we must address ourselves to answering this basic kind of question.

The experience gives rise to the symbol.   In general, all experience
gives rise to symbols of some sort, but some experiences are so pregnant with
drama that they seem to demand special symbolic handling. Furthermore,
some people are better at symbol-making than others, and create works of
interpretative art that sometimes endure for centuries. The originating
artists of religious ethics seem to have been people of that type, whose intense
human experiences were transformed into imaginative canvases of symbols
that direct our attention to the presence of the ultimate as the really signifi-

cant dimension of life. Or they may have symbolically pointed up a certain problem in mens' dealings with each other, or yet a certain quality that ought to be present in human life, like justice or love. When they uttered, or otherwise demonstrated their interpretations they gave us what might be called "first-instance theologies," that is, fairly spontaneous and non-reflective interpretations of events intensely experienced.

This may be illustrated with a quotation from Sidney Mead, taken from a work in which he attempts to demonstrate how America's early colonists were convinced that God had brought them to this land of promise.[1]

> Their sense of destiny is deeply rooted in the formative experiences of a people. But the important thing is the interpretation of the experiences—that subtle combination of insight into, and articulation of the meaning of the experience that is so deeply persuasive and widely accepted that it becomes a part of the common consciousness and passes into the realm of motivational myths. The experience of the Hebrew people in breaking away from Egypt, crossing the Red Sea, and entering into the land of their own was striking enough to be celebrated in song and story. But the important thing was that this happened to a people who had it in them to translate the experience into "the exodus." That made the difference between a successful rebellion of an obscure people, and the myth of a chosen people that through all subsequent history has remained a pillar of fire by night and a cloud by day.*

We should note that not all of the keenly felt experiences are so communal as was that of the Hebrews. Some, in fact, are highly personal, like the enlightenment experience of the Buddha, or the conversion experiences of Saint Augustine. Yet, in both communal and more personal events, the activity of creative symbolical interpretation is operative. And, if we are to understand the origins and formulations of a religious ethic, we must come to some provisional position on what happens in both the individual and the community experiences.

To do so let us approach the issue from two points of view, namely, that concerned with the quality of the event, and the other interested in the quality of the interpreter. From the first viewpoint, we can say that some events are so dramatic that they capture a person's attention, fire his imagination, and permanently alter his way of looking at life. The exodus for the Jewish interpreters, the death-resurrection event for Christians, the revelations Allah entrusted to Muhammed, and the *satori* experience of the Buddha are examples of such extraordinary occurrences. It is just such an event-centered focus that H. Richard Niebuhr brings to the forefront when he

* Sidney Mead, *The Lively Experiment* (New York: Harper & Row, Publishers, 1963), p. 75.

defines revelation,[2] and that Alfred North Whitehead employs when considering the concrete images that are cast up by such events in the making of religion.[3] Even more ordinary people like you and I have had experiences which are so forceful that we still remember them, and frequently use them to interpret what is happening at the present moment. In yet another significant area, we might note how frequently the experiences associated with Hitler's rise to power are being mentioned today when many Americans are alarmed by signs of national willingness to tolerate repressive measures against dissenters.

However, it would be erroneous to emphasize the importance of the event and neglect its interpreter. For events do not automatically give rise to symbols. Revelation is the work of an interpreting spokesman sizing up the significance of what is happening. In order to understand the constructs of symbols that we see in "first-instance theology" we need attend to the interpreter as well as to the experience. What would an exodus be without a Moses or a revelation from Allah without a Muhammed? When events occur, there are people either witnessing them or making them happen, and some of these people also interpret the events for themselves and their fellow human beings. They can be called people who are peculiarly sensitive to the human quest for fulfillment and liberation, and are quick to spot situations that have a bearing on this quest. Consider, for example, the way Dietrich Bonhoeffer was attuned to the significance of Hitler's moves in Germany or the way Dan Berrigan feels the pulse of the military-industrial establishment in America today. Deeply concerned about self and others, and the ambiguities and contradictions of the human condition, men like these come forth with symbols that communicate what we all more or less feel. Whether in their style of life, or in their teachings, they provide exemplary images, paradigmatic embodiments of attitudes and actions that suggest how we might cope with our present life.[4]

To say this is not to take sides with Carlyle's interpretation of history as basically the history of great men, but rather, to note that, along with significant events in history, we must also consider the importance of the people who interpret their significance. The lives of these people are frequently parables in themselves, raising them to the status of representative men or women. But they have also given us mosaics of imaginative symbols which make some sense out of contradictory and absurd experiences and point a way through life's labyrinth for others as well as for themselves. Yet, only a few of these symbolical mosaics, or "first-instance theologies" remain as truly influential forces in the cultures of our day. And those which have endured seem to have come from people who led unusually authentic lives, free from facile alternatives such as shallow conformity or raucous rebellion. They seem to have been people capable of embracing fully the paradoxes of being human, bringing life and teachings together into coherent sets of symbols that can only be called works of art. Well-lived lives cast in well-told stories are the first-instance examples of religious ethics. Thus, we can identify the simplest roots of religious ethics as memorable experiences made more memorable still by their sensitive interpreters.

These, then, are two aspects of the experiences which give rise to religious symbols. There is not only the event itself, but also its interpreter, the one endowed with the "gift of meaning,"[5] the meaning-maker who provides perspective for others as well as for himself. However, there is still a third aspect of first-instance theology which demonstrates the more specifically ethical dimension of religious interpretation. And that is the part of religious insight which focuses primarily on action and offering guidelines for behavior.

There seems to be a common pattern in all religions that is most clearly evidenced in the Jewish and Christian traditions of proclamation and instruction. When the religious meaning of any moment in history is proclaimed, it is generally followed by advice as to what would be considered a fitting response. In fact, it is probably a very common human pattern. For example, we would find it strange indeed if the civil defense declared a state of emergency, such as the threat of a tornado in the area, and did not follow up with appropriate instructions to the populace in the vicinity of the danger. And this is what we find in those moments of intense human drama when people assign a meaning to the experience and then suggest kinds of behavior that are fitting responses. The religious expression of this human pattern can be seen in the simple device used by both Jews and Christians. From the model event interpreted as the exodus to the present day, the religious teachers of Judaism have artistically interpreted the human condition (*hagaddah*) and have followed up with practical advice about suitable behavior (*halakha*, which includes all the various forms of *torah*). In the hagaddic proclamations, Jewish teachers provided declaratory meaning, assigning symbols of slavery, freedom and hope to the experiences of mankind. In their halakhic instructions they offered both illuminative and prescriptive meaning, promoting the pursuit of the declared meaning in various concrete and stylized forms of behavior. For example, the Jews were commanded at one period to give every slave a sabbatical because it was appropriate to the meaning of their former condition as a once-enslaved, but now freed people.[6]

We find that, at least in the New Testament, Christian writers adopted the same device, which then became known by the greek titles, *kerygma* and *didache*. Mark's account of the beginning of Jesus' public ministry is a classical example: " 'The time has come' he said 'and the kingdom of God is close at hand. Repent and believe the Good News.' "[7] We find it again in the author of the letter to the Ephesians who tells the Christians there that they have a new life in Jesus and should behave in such a way that this is obvious to all.[8]

It is the latter part of the two fold device which points to a specifically ethical dimension in religious symbols. It seems that the religious interpreters have not settled for simply the declaration of meaning, but have also gone on to indicate ways in which behavior can be suited to the situation. In the didactic movement of religious interpretation a way is pointed out, advice is offered, and a particular way of pursuing meaning may be prescribed. This is the function usually designated as ethical. It is the setting out of directives or norms which most people associate with ethics, but this is by no means completely independent from the first procedure in which meanings are proclaimed. For the instruction depends upon the statements declaring the general meaning of the situation and the role man is to play in it. This, however, will be discussed in considerable detail in following chapters. For the present, it suffices to note that when experience gives rise to the symbol we have at least three aspects which establish the specific meaning of the symbols of religious ethics, namely: the event, the interpreter, and the didactic part of the interpretation.

The symbol gives rise to thought.* The reactions of people to the cues provided in religious symbols are indeed varied, and relative to their capacity to use them. For some the reaction will be a fairly immediate alteration of physical activities or feelings. Others, however, will react by finding in these symbols reasons for reinforcing or altering their judgments about life. When performing this latter task religious thinkers are doing what is called theology. Hence, we can say that works of art get people thinking, especially when they are symbols produced by people who provide cues about the ultimate significance of life. These symbols often contain elements of universality, or recommend a general attitude or type of response that reverberates with the experiences of most men. They often interpret the human condition in such a way that they invite us to distill generalized notions from their very particularized details. Consider, for example, how the exodus of the Jews can be transposed from the unique particulars of that special event to more generalized notions of freedom and liberation. And the reason for this capacity in some religious symbols is that the experience or artistry of some persons or communities is so basically human that it perenially provokes thought about the fundamental human issues which were originally expressed in signs peculiar to very limited historical and cultural circumstances.

Religious symbols not only stimulate thought. They stimulate different types of thought, or different kinds of theologies. We can distinguish between at least two basic forms of theologizing, such as the more concrete and readily communicative "first instance theology," and the more reflective and

* Paul Ricoeur, *The Symbolism of Evil*, (New York: Harper & Row, Publishers, 1967), pp. 6, 354.

rationally organized theologies of "succeeding instances." In its first instances theology more closely resembles oral or written communications that are very close to the originating experiences, such as the sayings of Muhammed, the Buddha, or Jesus, at the time of, or shortly after, key events in their lives. Succeeding instances of theology stay rather close to the concrete and dynamic imagery of the first-instance, and only gradually depart into more reflective and rationalized treatments. The well-told stories of the Christian evangelists and Abu Bakr's collection of the sayings of the prophet Muhammed are samples of succeeding theologies that remain extremely close to the concrete symbolism of the original endowment of the founding interpreters. But the reflections of the Christian John on the themes of light and life, represent instances of a theology which moves toward more intellectualized forms of communication. Therefore, the one who tells the originating story, the first-instance theologian, is the one who gives the original set of symbols a definite shape, creating a coherent sign that will give rise to further thought and succeeding theologies. As thought and reflection move further away from the original creation, we find a progression of theologies that likewise moves from the spontaneously communicative to the more indirect and abstract signs of life and language.

To make this point exceptionally clear we might consider the following examples from Greek theology in the first millenium B.C. The pioneers who settled the Greek peninsula were hearty individuals who faced the usual number of frontier. challenges. The interpreters of their behavior singled out some who were extraordinarily robust individuals who surpassed the normally accepted limitations of human strength and courage. They memorialized these heroes in legends about gods and men engaged in contests with nature, human enemies, and with forces warring within the human heart. Then came Homer, who took those legends and told them in a coherent way, eliminating some of the discrepancies between different traditions of the same story, such as the different versions of the activities of the hero Achilles. He likewise took the body of disparate descriptions of the gods and organized these beings hierarchically under one supreme ruler, Zeus, in an elaborate scheme of activities centering on Mount Olympus. Homer was not the "first-instance" theologian of the symbols he organized, but rather one of the most notable theologians of the "succeeding instances." He should be identified as a theologian very close to the original and concrete imagery of the first-instances, responsible for gathering substantial parts of the *corpus* of legend into a few well-told tales, like the *Iliad* and the *Odyssey*. Having done this, his work then became a launching pad for succeeding instances of Greek theology, in which the symbols were used in a progressively more reflective manner.

We can trace this progress in Greek theology from the epic poetry of Homer, through the plays of the dramatists, concluding with the highly reflective work of the philosophers. There is a wealth of suggestive material across the whole spectrum of the progress, and some will want to question whether or not it should be called "progress" or "decline." However, I do not wish to address myself to all the possible issues involved in such matters, but do wish to focus your attention on at least one instance of revision in the art of religious ethics, since an understanding of the reconstructive skill is an important goal of this book.

Let us consider the *Oresteia*, the trilogy of plays done by Aeschylus, in which the author both perpetuates and revises Homer's theology of the activities of the gods. It seems that Aeschylus did not find it necessary to deny the role of the gods, as Euripides did, but was content with adding to the Homeric endowment, giving the gods a function suitable to the newer understandings of justice proper to a later time in Greek history. Orestes is portrayed as the symbol of a transition in Grecian understanding of justice and its processes. He kills his murderous mother, is pursued by the Furies, the consciences of the older household law of blood revenge, and is finally aided by Apollo and Athena. These younger members of the Olympian hierarchy inaugurate a system of trial by jury, act as defense attorneys for Orestes, and win acquittal for him from a group of his peers who have been asked to judge him rationally and not on the basis of fearsome totems and taboos from a more superstitious past.

While the Homeric tradition is respected in this story, it is also creatively transformed. The gods are taken seriously, but are given credit for promoting a new style of justice suitable to the government of a city, dissuading the citizens from their older convictions about the tribal code of blood revenge. The Furies, relentless female nags of the human conscience, are retained but transformed into *Eumenides*, gentle spirits, and their femininity is portrayed as a source of consolation rather than terror. In these and several other artistic symbols we can find a very substantial re-working of the theology which had given meaning to much of Grecian civilization. It is not very far removed from the kind of theology Homer did, but is a good example of a more reflective treatment of the spontaneous symbols coming from the first-instance legends.

Thus it is a very illustrative example for a study in religious ethics, since it focuses on the ethical aspect of the art of interpretation. But it also reverberates with our present sensibilities, focusing as it does on developments in moral awareness.[9] For example, the Orestean transition from household codes to more rational political justice strikes William Hamilton as a possible paradigm for our day. He sees Orestes rejecting his mother and taking on the radical insecurity of a hero who suddenly becomes responsible for an unprecedented set of decisions and actions. Such, for Hamilton, is the situation of theology in the west today. It is a theology which has come of age, and, in this era of the death of god, should become Orestean. It should reject the attitude of Oedipus in search of his lineage, and move out into the risky arena of unprecedented situations.[10] Others, using similar statements coined from Dietrich Bonhoeffer (such as, come of age, responsibility, forsakenness), draw upon the writings of the nineteenth-century German philosopher, Friedrich Nietzsche, for whom Aeschylus was a valuable model. Nietzsche believed that Aeschylus represented the culminating point of what he considered Greece's "real" golden age, because he was one of the last Greek artists who could be called "aesthetic men," that is, men who acknowledge life as basically tragic but overcome this tragedy through art.[11]

There is yet another angle to the story of Orestes which helps us understand both the developments in the art of religious ethics and our own present dilemmas. This is a story of rebellion, by both Orestes and the younger gods. It does not quite support the more traditional "system," but neither does it create anarchy in its place. It is a story endorsing justice by promoting an alternative to the conventional form of achieving it. To that extent it speaks to present concerns, and also points up something important in the developments that occur along the line of succeeding religious interpretations of human behavior. The *Oresteia* has a quality that makes it elusive for the powers that structure social and political life. It may well have been useful in legitimating the jury system of criminal justice, but that very system acts as a lever against the oppression of the weak by the strong. The quality possessed by the story of Orestes, and not always present in many examples of succeeding instances of religious ethics, is its ability to inspire hope. It does so because it places a high value on man and takes a view of history that looks to the future as open possibility, recommending that man take a hand in shaping what will occur. Contrast this interpretation, if you will, with the one given by Sophocles in *Oedipus King*, where we find a warning about the fate of those who dare to ignore the divine oracles. Man is there portrayed as a captive in a web of deterministic fate, where history is circular or freighted with obstacles, and the recommendation is to cooperate or be crushed.[12]

Many examples of religious ethics in more rationalized forms are like the story of Oedipus. We might also note the *Aeneid* of the Roman poet Vergil or the *Brahmanas* of India, which provided respectively, the inspiration for the dictatorial empire of Roman civilization, and the caste-oriented ranking of people in Hindu society. Abundant examples of a totemic or closed-type system of life endorsed by religious interpretation are also available in Christian history. But they would only serve to reinforce the point that succeeding instances of theology are not all cut from the same cloth, and can be discriminated on the basis of their ability to inspire hope or fear. By singling out this characteristic I hope to highlight two points. First of all, we can thereby more readily understand why some interpretations of religious ethics are more endurable than others. For those which inspire hope

seem to be more generally useful to larger numbers of men over longer periods
of time, while the interpretations that are easily manipulable by institutions
are repulsive and readily forgotten. Secondly, we can utilize this criterion in
the last section of this study, when the emphasis will be on developing more
skill in criticizing and reconstructing the key interpretations of our life today.

Thus far we have identified two steps in the development of a religious
ethic. We have considered originating events and interpreters, and some of
the dynamic forces involved in fostering succeeding reinterpretations of the
original works of art. Our attention must now turn to the third step in which
we will consider the institutionalizing of religious ethics.

Thought gives rise to plans and procedures.   We have seen how
imaginative symbols arise as one interprets experience, and how thought
and theology issue forth from these artistic signs. We must now consider how
plans and procedures frequently cap the process and harness the power of
developments taking place in religious ethics. A good example of such
occurrences can be seen in the fact that inspiring symbols of freedom gave
birth to democratic philosophies of politics and eventually were harnessed
by governmental institutions attempting to actualize these schemes. Similar
things happen to religious visions of human behavior, generating rationalized
theologies, which are capable of being structured in concrete patterns of
ritual and discipline, and sometimes are built into much larger entities like
entire cultures.

In fact, the distance between first-instance theology and institutionalized
religion is very short. The record of religious history reveals the interesting
insight that most world religions developed practical structures within, or
shortly after, the lifetimes of their inspirational founders. Judaism's tribal
federation was a short step from the desert community gathered around
Moses. The *Sangha* of Buddhism, the *koinonia* of the early Christians, and the
religious polity forged in Arabia by Islam's "rightly-guided caliphs" were
fast on the heels of the Buddha, the Christ, and the Prophet.

As the believing community expands numerically and geographically
the free-floating set of meanings where revisions are easily handled settles
into more universal creedal and disciplinary formulae. The symbolic artistry
of pioneer meaning-makers develops into a language, a stabilized set of
meanings, and, at least in the western hemisphere, into a Roman-like set
of universal rules. This phenomenon can be partially understood in terms
used by sociologists to explain the processes of institutionalization. As
described above, the religious interpretation of human behavior has gone
through three steps identified in sociology.[13] It has *externalized* meaning
(experience gives rise to the symbol), and *objectivized* a fundamentally subjective reality (the symbol gives rise to thought). The third step is the one
taken by the institution's newcomers or initiates, who *internalize* the symbols
in their objectivized form and make them their own.

The people who play the key roles in this institutionalization process usually understand that what they are doing is quite provisional, intended to firm up present accomplishments and provide a platform for future operations. They realize that they have not encompassed all of the meanings and possibilities in the artistic symbols which they objectify in plans and procedures for institutionalized living. In fact, they are well aware of the selectivity they employ in choosing certain key symbols while, temporarily at least, ignoring others. And all of this seems inevitable if we choose to create rational and orderly forms of living out of the highly diverse and sometimes contradictory meanings that are latent in a set of symbols rising from the experiences of one or more founding interpreters.

However, problems arise with the passing of time and the addition of youngsters and newcomers to the institution. These people need to be initiated and are taught to identify events in certain typical signs proper to the institution. This prejudices much of their future experience with a bias in favor of the institution's normal interpretation of all such events. Furthermore, the thoughts that have arisen from the originating symbols tend to get into ruts, and some are considered more "orthodox" than others, with the result that certain kinds of questions are discouraged. Such seems to have been the case when golden-age Greeks asked the totally predictable questions about virtue, or when Hindus of the classical periods asked what was required by one's caste duty. These are the kinds of predictable questions which institutions are prepared to meet. They can satisfy recurring basic needs and create predictability in many otherwise unnerving experiences of human life.

Problems arise, however, due to the fact that not all people are equally credulous, and even those who have strong commitments of faith need to understand how these commitments make sense. Hence, religious institutions begin to experience the need to explain and justify both creed and code to youngsters, converts, and those rare adults who continue to ask basic questions. Part of the problem lies in the fact that newcomers simply cannot experience the excitement latent in symbols that spoke eloquently centuries ago. Furthermore, many newcomers are not introduced to the original symbols at all, but are given the rational constructs which arose from them. But lack of enthusiasm provokes institutions into procedures of legitimation. They attempt to make the original dynamisms objectively available and subjectively plausible to the novices. And, when legitimation is a large preoccupation for a group, most of its thinkers get bogged down in the business of explaining and defending the faith. Theology becomes a convenient tool in the hands of the official legitimators, and generations of theologians become slaves to the system, and begin to look like sterile proclaimers of orthodoxy rather than creative thinkers.

Creative artists do come along, however, and begin to challenge the impressive construct of the symbolic universe created by the institution, as Buddha challenged Hinduism. Some create entirely new sets of symbols that are at odds with the original set from which the institution arose. Others simply reemphasize aspects of the original set. They highlight points that have been forgotten or ignored while the planners were busy emphasizing one or more points of order. Not all of these challenging artists are threatening to the institutionalized forms of religious ethics, but those who are will usually be met with devices of ostracizing or therapeutic rehabilitation. It seems that, once the original planners are gone, the institution's custodians lose sight of the provisionality of the plans and procedures and now mistake the impressive construct built on incomplete clues for the whole truth. Consequently, many creative artists are written off as mere "rebels" and their attacks are matched with procedures for liquidating all contrary interpretations through censorship or harassment. The net result is that in some cases, the art of ethical insight degenerates into an elaborate mantle of prescriptions protecting the self-serving interests of the institution. Ethics is reduced to law or sets of laws, fully sanctioned by the organization's god.[14]

I suppose we could say that the above description is obviously an example of an institution going perfectly crazy, or that it is the best account of the worst that can happen when artistic symbols go from thoughts about them to plans and procedures built atop. Yet, this surely does occur in all institutionalized forms of human living, to a greater or lesser degree.

To clarify the processes we have been discussing, let us consider a somewhat hypothetical case of institutionalizing. Suppose we are longhaired men living in a warm southern climate, never shaving or trimming our locks, and putting up with all the discomforts that would be ours. Then one of our friends suddenly cuts his hair and shaves his beard and appears so comfortable to us that his symbol inspires imitation. Some follow suit immediately, while others dislike him intensely. But still others get thinking about it and construct a "theology of hair" which explains how healthful this new practice can be. After a while our civic leaders set up barber shops and suppliers for them, create cleaning and grooming compounds, and invest the whole industry with the honorific title of "man's healing community."

Problems arise, however, when, generations later, our youngsters wonder why they must adopt this unnatural habit, or when aliens from the north, with full heads of hair, move into our close-cropped culture. If the institution is to survive, these idiosyncratic individuals must be dealt with, or their symbols may catch on and inspire contradictory institutions. So we can educate them, or, if that fails, harrass them, or finally penalize them if they still fail to cooperate.

When such a situation develops reforming efforts are sure to crop up. Sensible people within the systems will try to accommodate the "different ones," and may note that the original symbol was, after all, a sign of relief and comfort. They may contend that the new long-haired types may well be both clean and comfortable, while simply employing methods other than the customary ones. The tonsorial officials may protest and bring forth the latest official statements from the Warm Climate Conference on Dandruff and Protein Deficiency in Long Hair. But, if there is to be any light along with the heated debates that ensue, people will begin appealing to the symbols and thoughts which generated the plans and procedures which are now in open conflict with alternative ways of doing things. Recourse to the rationale and story behind the institution is both necessary and desirable. For what happens in the course of this investigation is that people discover both how they got where they are, and that where they are is just one possible location among several alternatives. They begin to see that in moving from the first clean-cut symbol to the present social system people had been doing a lot of selective interpreting. The older generations read the clean-cut sign as a symbol of comfort or health, but the younger group sees it as a sign of freedom. The officials who promoted the institution saw it as a possible means of economic health for themselves and their community. Many other slightly divergent stories will turn up in the investigation, and questions will arise about which one is the correct one, the right one, or the one to which we ought to give priority.

This hypothetical example may help us see that the institutionalizing stage of religious ethics caps and harnesses the energies latent in the symbols and the thoughts generated by them. The last stage concretizes one or more aspects of a multi-directional artistic symbol. This action is both a boon and a bane for the people who inherit the institution. On the one hand, it is a decided advantage to have these great human symbols made accessible to us, and to have our lives made somewhat predictable. But, on the other hand, it is disadvantageous to inherit an institution which distills all the possibilities of these great symbols into just one concrete form of life. Thus it is that institutionalized forms of religious ethics give comfort to some people while creating great disappointment in others. Some will find the concretized forms of love or caste-duty very clear and know just what they must do. But others will find these very specified forms of behavior too limited or out of touch with their present need. Hence they will either reject the ethic or try to transform it. In either case they will probably try to criticize and reconstruct the current official policy. They will find it supported by one or more official stories, and will then proceed to examine and test these stories evaluating them on the basis of some set of criteria. The problem is: Which criteria should they use?

ITS EVALUATION

"Our story vs. their story". The discussion of which story or set of moral values is best frequently turns out to be a totally partisan pitting of one position against another. Fully detailed styles of life and systems of ethics square off in their full-dress institutionalized uniforms. The supporters of each side are rallied around easily identifiable flags, such as the old and the young, students and administration, Catholics and Protestants, fundamentalists and liberals.

When searching for a criterion by which to evaluate the merit of some value story, people frequently do not get much farther than taking sides with the story to which they have some emotional commitment. It may be family, church, town or nation that is the object of the tie, but whatever its object, it is always some ideal whose triumph people will promote and whose defeat they will not tolerate.

The history of religious ethics is woven with an equally dialectical thread. A forceful stand taken by one theologian in favor of prayer is inevitably met with a reaffirmation of the importance of action. A stress on justice elicits a counter stress on mercy. An institution which emphasizes the value of detailed prescriptions occasions an opposing establishment with very general, non-prescriptive, guidelines. In short, the pitting of one position against another gives religious ethics the appearance of the pushme-pullyu animal from the story of Doctor Doolittle.

In the course of history it seems that the principal criterion employed by some positions is simply that all contrary positions are totally erroneous. Such a judgment is not very hard to come by if we rate all other positions in relation to the standard that claims ours is the "true" position. While this may bolster up an otherwise insecure community, it also closes it off from the invigorating experience of having its position challenged in open debate, and offers little enlightenment to people who are not fully partisan to that community's commitments.

There is yet another foundation for those who adhere to this criterion, especially in the contemporary form of power struggles between conflicting systems of thought and behavior. Much of the current popularity of the dialectical criterion is due to a pervasive belief in relativism. In its milder form this belief holds that values differ from culture to culture, and are relative to the experiences and conditions in those cultures. In its more vigorous generalized form, this belief holds that all values are completely arbitrary and irrational, and that they can be understood only in terms of the power that maintains them in force. Logically then, those supporting this more vigorous form of relativism will pit power against power, institutionalized form against alternative institutions, and will do the task of criticizing and reconstructing in terms of confrontation and revolution, because values are *relative to nothing*.

The "right" story.   Even if some are convinced that values are relative to nothing, we still hear the voices of those who contend that they have the right story, or those who continue to believe that there must be one such story and will strive to find it. These people may admit some milder forms of relativism, but contend that values and value-stories are *relative to something*. Just what that "something" is will be quite diverse but it is employed widely enough to merit some áttention in our discussion of evaluation criteria.

We can divide the claimants of and searchers for the right story into two general categories: those emphasizing the consistency between their story and the sources of it, and those who are concerned with the consistency of their story in terms of the effects it produces. (a) *The sources position* rests on the conviction that there is in fact one correct story about man and his behavior which can be discovered, verified, and, if necessary, reworked in terms of correspondence between the story and its sources. In its most plausible forms, this position usually attempts to keep statements of ethical values in correspondence with certain collections of relevant data. Zoologists will object when we come up with proposals for human behavior that conflict with what we know to be some of man's physical limits. The relevant set of data there may be highly precise limits of physiological abilities to walk a certain distance in a single day. School regulations requiring students to walk thirty miles per day would be considered inconsistent with this data, and, therefore, incorrect. The ethical stories told by religionists are frequently kept consistent with some traditional and normative set of data. It may be the Bible's commandments for fundamentalist Christians, or the Muslim treasury of rules from the Qu'ran, or the general statements of the classical eight-fold path of Buddhism. Whatever the accepted norm may be, all stories of ethical behavior in that tradition are frequently checked for correspondence between them and their model patterns.

This criterion has been used extensively in the religious ethics of the western world, and has profited many in their attempts to rework systems of ethics in their institutionalized forms. For, it provides a lever with which to pry the sometimes frozen teachings of religious ethics loose from their moorings, invoking the presumed commitment of the whole group to be faithful to some originating interpretation on which they were founded. For example, it has often been sufficient for Christian ethicians to simply point out that a particular statement in ethics is "not biblical" thereby undermining its worth for Christians. Often enough, however, these same ethicians employ another criterion such as that of orthodoxy, noting inconsistency between current ethical commentary and the declared positions of some great religious mind like Luther or Calvin. This concern about "true teaching" (*ortho-doxia*) seems to be contemporaneous with the institutionalizing of religious vision and thought. The standard of truth often turns out to be simply one historical moment's official interpretation of the original set of multi-directional symbols offered by some artistic religious interpreter. Hence, by using the correspondence-with-the-sources criterion, many religionists have been able to criticize and rework the ethical stories of their tradition, by questioning the degree of consistency between the prevailing system and its sources.

This type of position is able to handle relativity in several moderate forms. It can admit changes in the course of history, and even contradictions, but takes each one as relative to something rather definite, namely the relevant collection of data from which all interpretations have supposedly arisen. It can call them all to judgment before the bar of the facts as presented in the accepted normative text or data such as the Bible. And it can acquit most errors as merely failing to come up with an adequate representation of a very diverse and difficult set of data. But the data remains as the anchor, and every additional interpretation is relative at least to it, and is not purely whimsical.

(b) *The effects position* is one other form of the "right story" criterion, which handles moderate forms of relativism in several different ways. There is a *personal* effects position, which evaluates the consequences of various ethical positions in terms of what it does to the benefits or difficulties to individuals who have followed a particular value-story, and relies heavily on the highly subjective and relative effects demonstrated in witnesses for its case. There is also a *social* effects position, which evaluates ethical systems on the basis of their ability to bring about good social welfare. The ways in which this welfare is determined are highly relativistic, but proponents of this position believe they have settled the discussion if they can point to common norms of well-being that apply at least to the particular community or culture for which they are concerned. Thus, any set of ethical values which has provided the kind of ordering and harmony desired by a particular community will normally be rated "right," at least in relation to that specific group.

The effects position is commonly stated today in terms of "relevance." Those wanting a fully contemporary set of values will usually invoke the effects criterion, either personal or social, and will estimate the worth of competing value-stories on the basis of whether or not they meet the needs and requirements of people living at this point in time. In some circles it is not even necessary to spell out the consequences, sufficing merely to declare things relevant or not, with rather immediate reactions to the declaration. In its more thoughtful usages, however, the relevancy criterion links up with the sources position, and reaches back into the original collection of normative data, and attempts to effect a correspondence between it and the present experiences and needs of contemporary man.

Thus far we have considered two moderate forms of relativism, both of which refuse to accept the judgment that all moral values are completely arbitrary and accepted only because of the power sustaining them. They both insist that values are relative, but are relative to something—either their sources or their effects! We are now in a position to consider another form of moderate relativism, which will be the viewpoint behind all that is contained in this text.

The "good" story.   In his series on the saintly detective Father Brown, G.K. Chesterton has Brown reveal his secret for tracking down criminals. He says his secret is that he himself was really the killer in all of those cases. By putting himself completely in the murderer's shoes, he was able to see himself doing those things, and knew immediately who the killer was. In this spirit he was able to avoid the snobbish pharisaical attitude adopted by some students of criminals and criminology, and was able to understand the criminal by walking around in his skin for a while.[15]

This is the spirit of the perspective referred to in the preface as the "detached within," the criterion of the student of religion, who is detached from the truth and value judgments of any particular religious ethic, and who attempts to think sympathetically within each one. In this spirit we must come up with a tool which renounces the absolute relativism of the dialectical (ours vs. theirs) criterion, and one which respects, but does not rely on consistency with the sources or consequences as invoked by the right story criterion. The task is to provide a way of comparing each instance of religious ethics with something, and, if possible, to find a way to compare all instances to something common without invoking truth claims or rating them on some scale of better and worse.

Furthermore, if one is to do a creditable job of evaluating religious ethics, a way must be found to assay all of the stages along the line of a developing ethic. In other words, we must find a tool by which to assess the merits of the first two stages (symbols and thoughts) as well as the highly rationalized final stage of plans and procedures generated by the art and thinking gone before it.

While the offer of any criterion to fulfill these astonishing tasks may seem to border on consummate pride and arrogance, I suggest that the good story criterion is both simple and cogent enough to do all of this with a measure of success. For the good story criterion looks to the story itself, and asks about the inner consistency of its elements as related to one another. It can apply to the simple artistry of initial interpretation, the networks of thought generated by the symbol, as well as to the institutionalized forms of plans and procedures rising up from these humble beginnings. And it can compare any instance of religious ethics, and yet all instances to something common to them all, namely to a pattern of inter-relationships which all of them contain.

This criterion posits a model of religious ethics as a patterned series of relationships between three factors; a religious teaching about world processes, about man, and about how behavior should be directed.

It tests all forms of religious ethics on the same basis. We do not ask if a particular notion of man is correct, but only if it is functionally consistent with its teaching about behavior and life processes. For example, a religious ethic which depicts history as determined and fatalistic, while at the same time portraying man as a self-determining free being, would be considered functionally incoherent on the basis of the good story criterion. The truth of either one of these factors could well be questioned, but the criterion by which they would be evaluated in this text is concerned only with the incoherence of the statements in their functional inter-relationship.

This kind of critical evaluation is barely tolerable for the partisan insider whose viewpoint is fashioned completely within the party's story, believing its truth claims and questioning all others. Nevertheless, evaluation from the position of the detached-within takes the partisan's symbols and truth claims seriously, but simply refuses to take them literally. It tries to assess these signs in terms of the story itself, without either giving them absolute credence or subjecting them to judgment according to a totally alien and scientific criterion. Hence, it seems that the viewpoint taken in the good story criterion is able to discern a good story from a poor one, or is able to say that some story has an incoherent set of symbols, yet all the time respecting the credibility that the story holds for its adherents.

Finally, by using such a criterion we can come to understand some of the patterns of religious ethics which prevail across the board, from west to east, in several different religious traditions. Without trampling upon the obvious differences of questions, attitudes and methods of procedure that characterize these different traditions, the good story criterion will enable us to see some of the commonalities that prevail when all human beings do what this model understands to be the functions proper to the religious interpretation of human behavior.

A Systems Approach

Before we attempt to apply this criterion to several samples of religious ethics from the major world religions, we must come to terms with the subtitle of this work, namely, "a systems approach." Some clarifications are necessary in order to understand both the source of the good story criterion and the meaning that is assigned to the phrase "a systematic inter-relationship of the factors in a religious ethic."

Meaning and source. Many contemporary humanists and social scientists find the language and procedures of systems quite distasteful, particularly because of the abuses of most recent bad history, as well as the connotations implying *status quo* or power elites. Hence, it may be helpful to remind ourselves of the meaning of the Greek word *systema* as that which is put together, or a composite whole. In this radical sense, no one would object to using "biological systems" to refer to our put-together composite-whole human bodies. And yet many would object to using systems language in reference to the constructs of religious ethics, hoping, obviously, to avoid excessively structured approaches to human behavior.

However, this language is quite acceptable in both its root sense and in the usage to which it is put in contemporary efforts to understand the inter-workings of composites, whether they be mechanical, organic, or interpersonal. Furthermore, my approach in this study is such that it focuses our attention on three different interpretations and the interworkings of these three factors in the composites we call religious ethics. Thus, the language and procedures of contemporary scientific studies on systems seems both an accurate and serviceable analogy.

In order to make the meaning of systems as used in this text perfectly clear, consider the following five characteristics which scientists generally assign to systems:

> 1. Systems consist of two or more parts, elements, or aspects with some functional relationship to each other.
> 2. Systems are usually subsystems of larger ones; hence, it is best to confine one's study to the smallest unitary system.
> 3. Control systems have within themselves regulatory functions for the control of variables.
> 4. It is usually possible to identify the input-output portion or aspect of a system. Most systems have more than one form of input accounting for their varied outputs.
> 5. Usually (but nearly always in regulatory systems) there is some form of feedback which may greatly modify the net output of the system.*

Of the five mentioned above, the first two characteristics are the most pertinent to this present study, since they identify a system as a functional inter-relationship of elements or aspects, and circumscribe the limits of this study to one small unitary system of the larger reality called a religious tradition. Therefore, when a religious ethic is called "systematic" in this study, it simply means that it has identifiable factors or elements which are functionally inter-related. In the same sense the foundation, walls and roof of a house mutually interact to form a specific structural unity, or the characters, plot and action of a play interact to provide dramatic unity. When applied to religious ethics, we are concerned with the ways in which recommendations for behavior, notions of man, and points of view about world process mutually inter-relate to form a coherent ideology or plan of procedure.

Furthermore, when studying religious ethics from this point of view, we will not be considering churches, communities, or any large social groupings

* V. Lawrence Parsegian, Alan S. Meltzer, Abraham S. Luchins, and K. Scott Kinerson, *Introduction to Natural Science, "Part One: The Physical Sciences,"* (New York: Academic Press, Inc., 1968), p. 186.

built around the core story called a religious ethic. While we will consider examples of ethical schemes from at least three different stages (symbols, thoughts, and plans) we will refrain from considering the larger systems built around these units. The effort here will be that recommended in the second characteristic, namely, to confine ourselves to the smaller elementary sub-systems, since the larger macrosystems can be understood only by employing the complex analogies of control systems and the intricacies of input, output and feedback relationships. Such matters should be considered in future studies, but would be too complex to handle in this text, with its more modest introductory goals. We may liken the systems approach to religious ethics in this initial study to the investigation of a single television set, postponing for a later date the consideration of more complex matters like the network broadcasting systems such as NBC, CBS, or ABC.

When dealing with the composites we call religious ethics, there seem to be three main factors in all the examples I have investigated. Let us call these process, people, and principles. The *process* factor is whatever answer is given to the question "how do you view the whole process of life and action?" It embraces answers which speak of goals as well as context, finality as well as the theater in which life's drama is played. In short, it is the interpretation given to both the dynamics and purpose of human life. The *people* factor is broadly and simply the meaning we assign to ourselves. Whatever we understand ourselves to be or intend to become constitutes the people factor. This understanding can be acquired through highly personal judgment or by means of belief in the judgment of others, or a combination of both. Taken as one of the factors in a religious ethic, it is roughly the equivalent of what some call moral anthropology. The third and last factor, the *principles* factor, represents whatever concrete and communicable statements may be made about values to be achieved in behavior. These statements can be general or particular, autonomous, heteronomous, or theonomous, depending on the preference expressed in the particular ethics. But, whatever the prevalent emphasis of these statements, they can be taken as a set and considered as a single factor.

Besides identifying the main factors in a religious ethic, a systems approach goes on to study what we call the "functional inter-relationship" of these factors. By *relationship* I would like to signify the position one thing has with regard to another thing. A man is called a son because he is being considered in terms of a life-giving father or mother. A living-room window is called what it is because of its position in terms of the house's floor plan. Some tax laws are made to promote an equitable distribution of the burdens of life together in society. The term *interrelationship* takes this basic meaning a step further to indicate reciprocity in the relationship. A son's relation to a father is a two-way street. A living-room window provides outside illumination to a given room of the house, but also enables those inside the room to peer out. A tax law may educate society's neophytes in the equitable distribution of responsibility, but, in turn, can expect to be the object of modifications worked by these same people when, as voters, they find a better way of structuring this responsibility. Finally, when things are designated as *functionally* interrelated, we intend to note that the reciprocal relationship is of a dynamic and active character, one in which changes in the one affect changes in the other. As Robert Frost put it in his poem *The Silken Tent*, a woman

> . . . *is loosely bound*
> *By countless silken ties of love and thought*
> *To everything on earth the compass round,*
> *And only by one's going slightly taut*
> *In the capriciousness of summer air*
> *Is of the slightest bondage made aware.**

Likewise, changes in a father's attitude toward his son occasion counterchanges in the son's attitude, making us aware of the way in which the two have been functionally interrelated all the time. Closing the drapes of the living-room window or painting the interior a brighter color bring similar insights about inside-outside reciprocity. The resentment, evasion and open rebellion of youth against certain tax laws would also produce an awareness of the interactivity between people and the laws which govern their common activities.

Advantages.   While this approach to the study of religious ethics should not be considered a replacement for other more traditional approaches, it has some key advantages not available in other procedures. Some of these were mentioned earlier in this chapter when considering the "good story" criterion. First and foremost, the systems approach provides a way of entering into any religious ethic sympathetically, investigating its factors and their interactions, and evaluating the degree of coherence between them. It provides the perspective of the "detached within," taking the ethic on its own terms, and yet evaluating it by means of a functional criterion which does not impugn its intentions and claims. Secondly, it offers a way of handling relativity in ethics, by considering the relationships of the principal factors to each other. They are considered relative to each other, and thereby demonstrate the mistake of the position endorsing absolute relativism. Thirdly, by concentrating on the factors and their reciprocal

---

* From "The Silken Tent" from *The Poetry of Robert Frost* edited by Edward Connery Lathem. Copyright 1942 by Robert Frost. Copyright (c) 1970 by Lesley Frost Ballantine. Reprinted by permission of Holt, Rinehart and Winston, Inc. With acknowledgements to the Estate of Robert Frost, and Jonathan Cape Ltd., publishers in the British commonwealth and Empire.

functions, we can discover the commonalities prevailing between all instances of a changing religious ethic, as well as the common patterns of ethics from historically and culturally different religions.

While the three advantages just enumerated are the principal aims of the approach to religious ethics taken in this text, they are by no means the only hoped-for objectives of the study. For, there are important, if only accessory, skills, which I hope this type of disciplined learning will bring to those who take it seriously. First of all, familiarity with systems language and procedures can facilitate communication between people trained in various disciplines, for this set of signs has become a cross-disciplinary vehicle for interpreting many aspects of human life. The input-output-feedback language originating in electronics is commonly heard in things as diverse as the ecology of biosystems and cities. There is, in fact, a high probability that systems language and thought patterns will be even more widespread as the jargon of the social and political sciences becomes part of the common treasury of everyday language. Therefore, it seems altogether appropriate for contemporary humanistic studies to be not only conversant with, but also able to employ systems' patterns of discovery and communication.

The second skill which can also be acquired through a study such as this is what I have referred to earlier as the twofold skill of criticism and reconstruction. While the entirety of the last chapter will be devoted to drawing out the reader's talents in this direction, it is important to call attention to these skills at this point, before we immerse ourselves in the interworkings of several systems of religious ethics, all of which may or may not be of pressing concern to us. What is of great moment at this time in history is the ability of each person to come to terms with a multitude of ideals and value stories, all of which are vying for the allegiance of the masses, and some of which are already very powerful over large numbers of people.

To take an example of something that was very important for college students during the sixties, consider the difficult time many had in deciding whether or not to endorse the story of the Students for a Democratic Society. This group's title sounds traditional enough, but its slogans and programs aroused considerable suspicion and animosity, with occasional efforts on the part of some to either repress its activities or to suppress the organization entirely. Few debated with the SDS publicly, and fewer still heard more than the slogans and news reports of its activities. As a consequence few ever took the time to critically evaluate the ethical stance of the SDS in the light of its charter documents and the thoughts which rose out of these symbolic declarations. Granted that it takes some effort to see the systematic connection between the tactics of this organization and their Port Huron statement on the meaning of man.[16] However, there not only is such a reciprocal tie, but an understanding of it is essential to any accurate evaluation of this radical student group. If investigated and evaluated on the basis of the "good story" criterion, both the friends and foes of the SDS would profit immensely, and would be better able to either agree or disagree with the complete scheme of thought supporting what we see on the surface.

Some familiarity with the tool of systems analysis as used here to illuminate the procedures of religious ethics should have as one of its by-products a keener sensitivity to the factors and interrelationships which prevail in all the stories that are put together on the theme of human behavior. By extending the powers of discernment and careful analysis acquired in this study, some may find help in both criticizing current offerings in moral values, and in the fashioning of more acceptable alternatives for the future.

STUDY QUESTIONS

1. Would you agree that religious ethics is a phenomenon which we can easily afford to ignore without much loss to the skills we need as human beings? If you do, is it because of the bad experiences you have had with particular forms of moral teaching from religious institutions? Could there be others more appealing and instructive with which you are not familiar?

2. Do you agree with this chapter's statements about events, interpreters and hopeful interpretations? See if it applies in writings like Daniel Berrigan, *False Gods, Real Men*, (New York: The Macmillan Company, 1969).

3. Do all religious symbols necessarily give rise to thought? Is it true that some religious traditions are opposed to thinking about matters of belief? Should thinking out the implications of faith be considered progress or decline?

4. Can you give an example of a number of "succeeding theologies" other than those mentioned from Greek religion in this chapter? Would the successive steps mentioned in this chapter hold true, for example, in the history of Hinduism, as its literature moves from the *Vedas* to the *Brahmanas* to the *Upanishads*?

5. Try to apply the notion "thought gives rise to plans and procedures" to matters like university curriculum, dormitory regulations, or the Sunday "blue laws" in some localities of the country.

6. See if you can apply the evaluation criteria given in this chapter to any current debate on foreign policy. Identify the normative and traditional policy, various reinterpretations of it, and the current administration's handling of it. Note any conflicts between the Congressional foreign affairs committee's understanding of the policy and that of the Secretary of State. Determine if possible which parties are using criteria which are (1) dialectical, (2) correspondence-orthodoxy, (3) functional.

7. You might want to note the difference between evaluations which are concerned with the "rightness of the act" and those focusing on the "rightness

of the story." A serious discussion of the following would be a good start: Paul Ramsey, "The Case of Joseph Fletcher and Joseph Fletcher's Cases," in his *Deeds and Rules in Christian Ethics*, (New York: Charles Scribner's Sons, 1967), pp. 145–225, especially pp. 185, 224–25.

8. See if you can find an example of a religious ethic in which there are no process-people-principles factors, or in which these same factors do not have reciprocal relationships.

9. Try to demonstrate how the systems approach mentioned in this chapter is "less humane" than other approaches, or how it lends itself to furthering the diminishing of man's value by structuring things too much.

NOTES

1. Sidney Mead, *The Lively Experiment* (New York: Harper & Row, Publishers, 1963), pp. 76–78.

2. H. Richard Niebuhr, *The Meaning of Revelation* (New York: The Macmillan Company, 1946), p. 93.

3. Alfred North Whitehead, *Religion in the Making* (New York: The Macmillan Company, 1926), p. 32 ff.

4. Cf. Maurice Friedman, *To Deny Our Nothingness* (New York: The Delacorte Press, 1968), pp. 18–27.

5. Cf. a chapter by this title, from which many of the above thoughts arose, in Richard Rubenstein's *The Religious Imagination* (Kansas City: The Bobbs-Merrill Co., Inc., 1968), p. 171 ff.

6. *Deuteronomy*, Chap. 15; Cf. also C. H. Dodd, *Gospel and Law* (New York: Columbia University Press, 1960), pp. 3–24.

7. *Mark*, I; 15.

8. *Ephesians*, 5: 9.

9. Cf. his The House, *The City and The Judge* (*The Growth of Moral Awareness in the "Oresteia"*) (New York: The Bobbs Merrill Co., Inc., 1962), p. 29 ff.

10. William Hamilton, "The Death-of-God Theology" in *The Christian Scholar*, Spring, 1965; cited in *The New Christianity*, ed. William R. Miller (New York: Delta, 1967), p. 336 ff. Cf. also Herbert Fingarette, "Orestes: Paradigm Hero and Central Motif of Contemporary Ego Psychology," in *The Psychoanalytic Review*, Fall, 1963.

11. John E. Smith, "Nietzsche: The Conquest of the Tragic through Art," in *The Tragic Vision and the Christian Faith*, ed. Nathan A. Scott, Jr. (New York: Association Press, 1957), p. 211 ff. Note: Albert Camus might also be mentioned in this context, particularly his essay on "Rebellion and Art" in *The Rebel* (New York: Vintage, 1965), p. 253 ff.

12. Cf. Charles Moeller, "Renewal of the Doctrine of Man" in *Theology of Renewal* (New York: Herder and Herder, Inc., 1968), II, 240 ff.; Cf. Also an essay on hermeneutics and structuralism by Paul Ricoeur in *Esprit*, No. 11 (1963), pp. 613 ff., esp. p. 616.

13. Cf. Peter Berger, and Thomas Luckmann, *The Social Construction of Realty* (New York: Doubleday and Company, Inc., 1967), p. 59 ff. (Chapters 2 and 3).

14. Ibid., p. 93 ff.

15. Cf. G. K. Chesterton, "The Secret of Father Brown" in *The Father Brown Omnibus* (New York: Dodd, Mead & Co., 1935), pp. 633–41.

16. *Port Huron Statement* (Chicago, 1966), pp. 6–7; Cf. also the same reprinted with permission in A. K. Bierman, and J. A. Gould, *Philosophy for a New Generation* (New York: The Macmillan Company, 1970), pp. 38–41.

chapter two

Process

IN THIS AND FOLLOWING CHAPTERS our attention will focus on the factors and interactions mentioned briefly in the first chapter. For clarity's sake, we shall consider each of the three factors in separate chapters, beginning with process and concluding with principles. When considering each factor, however, we will also be concerned with the network of interconnections between it and the other two factors. As we move through discussions of all the factors in this fashion, we should be able to accumulate a fairly complete picture of the functional interrelationships of process-people-principles in the samples of religious ethics chosen for our consideration in this book.

You will note that, in this and in succeeding chapters, an effort has been made to provide samples of several different traditions of religious ethics. The reasons for this are several, among which you should include: (1) an effort to begin or enrich your familiarity with some of the principal traditions of religious ethics from both the East and the West, and (2) an attempt to demonstrate the common elements and patterns which are shared by the ethical teachings of all major world religions.

The present chapter begins this study in earnest by drawing your attention to what may be the least mentioned, but nonetheless important, factor in religious ethics, namely, the process factor.

The Meaning
of the Process Factor

The factor we call process may be more familiarly known as end, purpose, or finality, depending upon the context in which a person has become acquainted with this notion. But each of the more familiar terms shares the common disadvantage of a long tradition of particularized connotations that may lead to a misunderstanding of the point being made here. Hence, the term process will be used to avoid this pitfall. Furthermore, it seems that the more familiar terms highlight just one aspect of what is encompassed by the meaning of process. They underline ends more than means, goals more than the contexts in which they are pursued, and, hence, are more restrictive than the broader connotation to be given "process" in this chapter.

The choice of the word process has more than the superficial advantages of alliteration with the terms people and principles. It also provides a more accurate identification of our present concern in the language of contemporary science and philosophy, both of which conduct much of their discussion in the process terminology popularized by Whitehead. Furthermore, talking about process allows us to embrace a wider variety of perspectives than the somewhat restrictive teleological terms mentioned earlier. For instance, it will be entirely in order to discuss as general a question as "how do you view the whole process of life and action?" By using the very general term process we can devote time to the context of human activity, the theater of the drama of human life, as well as considering the goal-oriented activities that finality symbols usually connote.

In getting at the meaning of his place in life's processes, man has had to answer certain recurrent questions throughout the course of his history. Time and again we have been faced with queries like: What are we involved in?, How did it begin and how will it end?, Is it meaningful, absurd, or capable of transformation?, What about our responsibility in the cosmos, and the range of our effective action?

Questions like these do not merely lie around on the periphery of our existence. They demand our attention in an effort to come up with at least provisional answers. Quite simply, it seems that we are unable to act in life's drama without some convictions about these matters, and are, therefore, pressed for some tentative replies. Granting that the answers will always be partial and open to revision, the issue cannot be skirted without working harmful effects on the one who has become aware of the questions. If, then, we choose awareness as opposed to some Walpurgis Night's Dream, we thereby decide to do what is imperative, namely, identify and begin to understand the general process in which we live and act.

Each and every view of the process in which we operate has certain constitutive elements. What follows is not an exhaustive listing of these elements, but, rather, the identification of the most common elements involved in a perspective on process.

Time and space. If we were to ask some elementary school child about his view of the world, he might treat us to a juvenile recital to the effect that "it's about time; it's about space." Puerile as is its form, it is, nevertheless, quite correct in pointing out that symbols of both time and space figure into every view of world process. Without spatial and temporal references there would be little or no understanding of the context of our life and action.

Take the matter of *space* for our first consideration. Space has to be symbolized in some way, and something of man's relationship to space needs to be identified or a person has no end of difficulties trying to accommodate himself and his activity to his surroundings. For instance, how would we manage without the simple spatial references like "here, there, up and down, left and right?" Simple denominations like these situate us and provide a way of handling minor matters of relationship. However, more complex matters require more sophisticated symbols (or the substitute simplicities agreed upon by the ordinary sense of communities). The orbital gyrations of the earth in irregular elliptical patterns around the sun demand a great deal more of our symbol-making skills, or are, by common convention, simplified in the sunrise and sunset substitutes of ordinary language.

However, the spatial element of a view of process involves more significant issues than simple references to lateral space and the space above and below. Space, as part of a view of process, must also include some reference to the *significance* of being above, below, or wherever. The simple references are a matter of correct observation, or correcting earlier views. Ptolemy located earth in the center of the universe, but Copernicus, armed with improved tools for observation, corrected the view to a heliocentric universe.

This correction of spatial references is by no means inconsequential. Whereas Ptolemy's contemporaries were able to symbolize man as the measure of all things in a geocentric universe, the contemporaries of Copernicus began to see man as a being clinging with the force of centripetal gravity to a ball erratically spinning around its galaxy's sun. This change in perspective is rightly called the Copernican Revolution, a transposition of man's significance, dethroning him from the center of the universe and depicting him as a being seemingly flung at random into an array of stars and planets.

The spatial component in a view of process is not merely a factual statement of observed relationships; it must also assign a *meaning* to these factual relationships. And that was the effort of the interpreters using the scientific facts flowing from the observations of Ptolemy and Copernicus. They indicated the meaning of spatial relationships in polyvalent symbols which point in several directions all at once, and open out to recurrent future reinterpretations (such as, "measure of all things," "flung at random"). While a view of process must necessarily contain factual observations, the interpretative symbols which assign meaning to the facts are by far the more significant constituents. It is interpretations more than facts that most clearly frame our dramatic consciousness of the particular kinds of signs which will occupy our attention in this study, since they are the ones most analogous to those used by religious views of life's process.

In a viewpoint on process, *time* acts as a correlative of space. Everyday conversation in the twentieth century is sprinkled with references to the shrinking size of the world, and the scientific inaccuracy of those statements goes unattended because of their significance. What is symbolized is, of course, a temporal relationship, namely, the decreasing amount of time required to travel to or have contact with people and events around the globe.

Since our concern is primarily with the meaning and context of human activity, the quantitative measuring of time and its resultant symbols are of less importance than human language designating the significance of time. An oversimplified polarization of viewpoints on time may bring this out. One pole of opinion about time may by termed "past-oriented," the opposite "future-oriented," and the mean position might be called that of being "oriented between the times." The first view sees the past as the most significant part of time, viewing everything that happens now in the light of the past. The second does something similar using the future as its focus, and the mean position takes upon itself the peculiar and uncomfortable tension of living with *both* memory *and* expectation.

In either case, it manifests the need we have for some expression of relationship to the meaning of past and future, and indicates the wisdom of a symbol that embraces the dialectical tension between them, instead of the counterposing symbols that elect one to the exclusion of the other.

Constancy and variability. Another set of correlative elements that go into the make-up of a process view is one that symbolizes temporal and spatial relationships in terms of their schedules of occurrence. Events not only occur; they frequently occur in the same place or at the same time of year or when people are at a certain age. When this is seen, constancy is identified and generalized statements become possible. County courthouses are the places where personal property taxes are paid. Springtime is cherry-blossom time. Adolescents suffer from acne and identity crises.

For every such generalized "constant" a particularized "variable" can be cited. *Our* courthouse sends the tax collector to the home. The frost destroyed the cherry blossoms *in Virginia* this year. *My* son was never troubled with acne infections when he was an adolescent. These examples illustrate the truism that every constant is but a summary statement about concrete and diverse variables. It always implies qualifiers such as "most, the majority of cases, and so on," but this implication is frequently either forgotten or ignored. Yet, there is one viewpoint about process that sees only the recurrent pattern in time and space. Everything, according to structuralist theories, is but an instance of the constant pattern, a particularized example of what, when or where the same things always occur. Hence, there's "nothing new under the sun" and everything is thoroughly predictable. However, sharply contrasted with this synchronous interpretation of time, is the conviction that everything is unique and eventful, a never-before happening. From this point of view, every occurrence has nuanced meaning, each person is totally unique, and there is no fully reliable advice to be had from the similar, but obviously not identical, experiences of others. Therefore, we are advised that there can be no true predictability in human life, nor is such even desirable.

Just like the temporal orientations toward past or future, the emphases on the constant or the variable can lead to either an artificial polarization, or a position of embracing their tension and of saying that this too is a matter of "both-and." However, whether in isolation or in combination, there can be no doubt that the correlative elements of constant-variable are always ingredients in any interpretation of process.

Chance and planning.   Closely related to the matter of constancy and variability are the symbols used to designate why something occurs at one particular moment and not at another. It may have been either planned that way or happened fortuitously. In fact, every happening can be seen as something intended, purely accidental, or a combination of both.

Primitive societies seem to incline toward interpretations that are fateful and fortuitous, depicting life as a hazardous venture under the capricious control of the deities. More complex societies experience some measure of control and evidence a more abundant set of planning symbols, such as "building empires, renewing our cities, planning alternatives for the future."

There is a functional connection between a future-oriented view of time, a preference for the unique and variable, and planning. In fact, they cohere so well that we can begin to see how elements accumulate in patterns to form coherent viewpoints on process. The same is obviously true of synchronous time, constancy and fate, which likewise become conjugated into fairly complete viewpoints about the context of life's process.

This very brief mention of chance and planning as common symbols in process perspectives will have to suffice for the present, serving principally to identify them as ingredients in the development of the aggregate set of interpretations called the process factor.

Vistas and horizons.   Another set of correlative elements constituting process schemes is one that concerns the question of the "range" of one's point of view. The terms vistas and horizons are used to indicate the broad and narrow bands on the spectrum of vision.

Some views of process take relatively little into consideration while others are extremely cosmic and overarching. The latter are like broad vistas while the former are relatively narrow in outreach. And it is not merely the difference between generalists and specialists that explains this. It is also a matter of how extensive a range of relationships the specialist perceives when he has not deliberately limited himself to a narrow one for moments of specialized inquiry or action. In other words, it is one thing to be a practicing gardener for moments of one's existence, and quite another to sum up human life exclusively in terms of lawns and shrubbery.

Everyone has both vistas and horizons, or, if you prefer, a set of relative horizons both wide and narrow. Presumably we cannot get along without either setting some limit or deciding that there is none. The point here is that vistas and horizons provide the reference points for the human landscape called process. They set out points of arrival and departure, catch light and cast shadows, permit topographical and cartographical descriptions of the context of human activity.

This landscape metaphor of process provides a way of saying that vistas and horizons are correlative elements in any "lay of the land" over which we move, symbolizing either a relatively large or small range of relationships for human activity.

Meaning: its loss and recovery. Student slogans in the sixties have employed the word "meaningful" in a variety of ways, applied it to courses in the universities, their relationships to people, to both work and leisure. Some of their elders find cause for concern in this, wondering what youth will do when they discover that what is presently meaningful may not be such ten years from now. Will they, some wonder, be able to recapture lost meaning, or transform the less meaningful into something worthwhile? Surely, too, there is cause for concern when human activities are set in polar opposition as either meaningful or absurd. In so doing we all fall prey to the myopia which sees everything in simplistic divisions of black and white, the clear evil and certain good.

And yet the concern is misplaced if it focuses exclusively on the young, for the issue of meaning has bearing on the activities of all men, and colors everyone's view of the process in which we are involved. We have only to think of the literature of existentialism, the theater of the absurd, and the appeal to revolutionary tactics in today's politics. There we find themes which have engaged contemporary man's attention because they deal with a loss of meaning in so many different areas of life, for adults as well as for youth.

The matter of meaning is, in fact, a human issue, involving both young and old, an issue absolutely central to the way we conceive our life in the world, and one that has a decisive bearing on our notion of the process. It is not, however, just another one of the common constituents mentioned in the preceding pages. Rather, meaning is more like the animating force in each of these elements. Time and space become constituents of a view of process precisely because they are assigned some meaning or significance. Although this was noted when dealing with the elements separately, it now merits more explicit attention from the previously unmentioned vantage point of losing and recovering meaning. Meanings come and go, and we are thereby confronted with the necessity of taking some stand on what is to be done.

Here again some extreme positions constantly reappear. One pole would be the view that there is never really any loss of meaning in life. What occurs, in this view of the matter, is a person's failure to remain faithful to the meaning of various things like education, job, and marriage. Hence, the only requisite is some type of return to the flock, a conversion to the meaning that has been there all along. The opposite pole, enjoying a great deal of prestige in this age of transition, claims that, since everything loses its meaning when you really face up to the facts, there is no real meaning at all (life is absurd), or there is only the meaning you make out of nonsense (some forms of existentialism). Here, then, life is revealed in its raw absurdity as waiting for Beckett's Godot, and meaning never comes. Consequently, relationships in this naked universe are illusory, for time is a twisted clock bent over a pointless chair in the middle of a room where space is neither here nor there.

Still another position is possible, however, acknowledging the decline and loss of meaning, but also firmly convinced that once lost meaning can yet be recaptured. In this position, activity neither irretrievably loses its meaning nor automatically yields it up. What is required, according to this position, is an *engagement* with absurdity, a wrestling with senselessness, and ransoming meaning from it.

The next section of this chapter will have something to say about the way religions handle meaning—lost and regained. For the present, then, suffice it to note that the matter of meaningfulness figures prominently in one's view of process, giving spirit and form to the way various symbols of the process are conjoined.

How Religious Interpretations
Help Shape These Process Elements

A few pertinent citations from the thoughts of Howard Warshaw will serve to introduce the content of this section:

> We live in a world of events that are essentially chaotic; we go
> through an infinite process of sensation; until these events are cap-
> tured in some form—language, mathematics, art—we have noth-
> ing . . . The first thing I'm interested in is in coming to grips with
> the kind of chaos I spoke of and finding an order in it. A painting
> that begins with this wild-goose chase for reality has the basic
> quality necessary to geniune art.*

* Reprinted by permission from the March 1969 issue of *The Center Magazine,* a publication of the Center for the Study of Democratic Institutions in Santa Barbara, California, p. 49.

Then, in drawing out his understanding of artistic activity, Warshaw notes how art helps shape our awareness of ourselves:

> If people realized that it is through art—now I'm talking about bad art, too—that we get our conceptions of what life is and that ultimately art puts us in touch with our own reality, they would realize how absolutely dependent on art they are. Every man has to have stories told to him, songs sung to him, pictures to look at. It is out of these artistic experiences that we shape the idea of what we are.*

However, one example of contemporary bad art is that of some advertisers. Like good art, bad art is a fiction, a man-made symbolization of something significant for mankind. Warshaw feels that, in the United States, advertising is the primary fiction of our day, quantitatively more omnipresent than any other art form, and because of its artistic poverty, also more potentially harmful than all others. The reason for this lies in the fact that advertising must justify its claims on man's attention while it appeals to his buying power. Therefore, in addition to painting products in appealing patterns of color and sound, it also manufactures general fictions about what the world is like and what it means to be a human being. Lies about products are thereby compounded with more damaging lies about life; creations, essentially destined to sell goods, become at the same time carriers of infantile and undesirable fictions which are far from being honest attempts to come to grips with the chaotic.[1]

A similar comment has been made by Albert Camus in his essays on rebellion, noting that rebellion can be observed in art as "in its pure state and in its original complexities."† Like Nietzsche, Camus posits a metaphysical urge for unity and coherence as the cause of the rebellion which becomes art. "In every rebellion is to be found the metaphysical demand for unity, the impossibility of capturing it, and the construction of a substitute universe."‡ Furthermore, in its rebellion, "art disputes reality, but does not hide from it."§ In other words, good art confronts the chaotic and creates a coherence that provisionally conquers absurdity, but never completely escapes it.

In this section an attempt will be made to show that the stories of religious traditions have functioned in a similar fashion. Like all art, they function as

---

* Reprinted by permission from the March 1969 issue of *The Center Magazine,* a publication of the Center for the Study of Democratic Institutions in Santa Barbara, California, p. 52.

† Albert Camus, *The Rebel* (New York: Vintage, 1956), Copyright (c) 1956 by Alfred A. Knopf, Inc., p. 252.

‡ *op. cit.,* p. 255.

§ *op. cit.,* p. 258.

general fictions about life in the world, or what is called *process* in this chapter. Those that have been good stories are those that had what Robert Frost called a lover's quarrel with the world. As all stories that have tried to create a unity out of chaos, the most durable and popular religious stories have been those that made an effort to overcome tragedy without fleeing from it.

However, the present atmosphere is one in which many men find the religious stories about the world irrelevant. Some more pejoratively consider them expressions of superstition and ignorance. Writing with a spectrum of opinion, ranging from indifference to open hostility, in mind, it seems important to note that the religious story has had a great deal of influence in the formation of what we now call the enlightened scientific understanding of the world. In fact, a book written recently develops the thesis that these very stories are still influential, albeit if only in the artifacts that civilization has built under their inspiration. For instance, religion in America, the thesis claims, has stirred successive embodiments of the American dream which were transformed into "profane" institutions. Religious teaching about the importance of education, morality in public life, the value of pluralism, equality and nationality continue to have a strong influence in this country, if not in their original form, then just as effectively in the institutions built to make these dreams come true. They have been transformed into achievements now belonging to the citizenry instead of being the sole prerogative of the saints.[2] Other examples could be drawn from the social transformation of the good Samaritan story into institutionalized forms of welfare, but enough may have been said to point up the value of studying the manner in which religion shapes our view of the world. It seems that the secular symbols common to all men are first sacralized and set aside as "religious," and then returned to the common marketplace as secular reality now transformed through the meaning-making mediation of religious artistry. Most of the elementary symbols of process, such as space, time, horizon, cosmos and chaos, have gone through periodic appropriations by religious thought, been assigned a sacred meaning, and have been returned to the secular domain in the form of concrete human institutions.

Yet, religion is not alone in the interpretation of life and its processes. There are many works of human artistry which shape our notions of what we are involved in. Generally there is no shortage of volunteers for the meaning-making task at any given moment of history. In both wartime and at times of peace, ministries of war and defense turn out worldviews by the thousands in numerous manuals of conduct and procedure. The "growing up absurd" tale that Paul Goodman told college students in the sixties became a vantage point from which they peered down on the flea circus and rat race that seemed to be apt descriptions for the activities of American society.

Thus, one might well ask what specific role religious interpretations of life might have. And an answer begins to appear in considering the difference between the interpretations of Goodman and the Pentagon, which more properly resemble myth-mongering, and those of some works of art that have taken more cosmic matters for their subject and have created a poetry about things that can be dealt with in no other way. Among these we would have to include great literature, which, in Camus' estimation, aims at the creation of a "closed universe or a perfect type."[3] Literature of this type reveals a rebellion against chaos and absurdity, the effort to relate ourselves to the basic realities in which we are involved. The process, the theater of our activity must somehow be portrayed or there is no effective way of relating to it, or living in it as actors creating its drama. Hence, literature (including religious literature) reveals the necessity of taking a stand on the nature and meaning of human activity, or, if you prefer, reveals the metaphysical urge for unity and coherence in life, a willingness to believe in a good story that functions as a means of relating to the hidden and the chaotic.

Religious *mythos*, the story-telling form peculiar to religion, like all human fictions of a general type, releases its meaning only to those who enter into the convention that finds it credible. Once having so covenanted, the story becomes less a mode of explanation than one of action for the hearer. It provides a way of relating to unknowns and paradoxes. Interestingly enough, this function of the religious story has ever been respected, while attempts to put the story forward as scientific explanation have always run into opposition and generated a loss of confidence in those trying to do so. However, when taken as functional, or as a set of symbols creating sense in absurdity, the religious story has shaped, and still continues to shape, peoples' awareness of the process that environs us. That will be the central point to be made in this section. The second, and related point, is that the religious story has been able to shape our awareness by virtue of the fact that it has artistically blended the constituent elements of process views as mentioned earlier, and brought them in a balanced view which takes issue with life without running away from it.

A number of examples of religious *mythos* about world process come to mind, but two general schemes stand out as the most prominent views of process shaped by religious interpretation. As these are detailed an effort will be made to point up the ways in which they utilize the elements of the process view put forward in the first part of this chapter.

The religious interpretations of primitive peoples are notably lacking in temporal references. The primordial *mana*, or being, is "everywhen" as well as everywhere. Relationships, even those using the symbol of "time," are cast principally in spatial terms. The horizontal relationships so common to us, where time is imagined as behind us and ahead of us, are expressed in vertical terms by primitives, whose effort is usually to bring the sacred and primordial time "down from above." This obviously represents some effort to symbolize process, but one which cannot square with the thinking of a literate people whose perspective is perforce much different from that of the primitives.

With the advance in the arts of living comes an historical sense and a parallel shift in the religious interpreting of world process. In advanced religions, that is those usually qualifying as both durable and widespread "world religions," we find two generalized schemes of world process, namely, the cyclical and the linear.

THE CYCLICAL

While this view is sometimes characterized as peculiarly "eastern" it should be noted from the start that the cyclical view was the view of the very western Greeks, and occasionally is found in some passages of the scriptures of western religions, as well as reappearing from time to time in the popular sense of westerners trying to understand what appear to be repeat performances of history.

We are not, therefore, trying to equate cyclical with eastern, and wish merely to note that the cyclical is that viewpoint on world process which depicts us as caught up in ever-recurring cycles of events. Although different, these cycles go on indefinitely, and cultures where this view prevails give evidence of little or no concern about absolute beginnings or endings. Things come and go, but they have always been doing so, and will continue to do so. These cultures have symbols of Oneness-in-eternal-Nowness and envision the possibility that man can break through the cycles, bringing the process to a halt for himself as one individual, but the context of his activity is, was, and always will be cyclical.

As examples, consider the Buddhist and Hindu schemes from the vantage point of the constant-variable set of symbols.

In Theravadan Buddhism,[4] the earliest and most conservative form of Buddhism, there are thirty-one horizontal planes of existence in which the upper eleven are beyond the vagaries of creation and destruction, while the lower twenty undergo successive cycles of new beginnings and new endings. Constancy and regularity occur in *both* the upper eleven imperturbable planes (whose dwellers descend to populate the lower levels at reconstitution time) *and* in the pattern followed in the lower twenty regenerating planes. In these latter planes beginnings are always bright, but gradually dim as the dwellers from above pick up more and more earth substance, growing conscious of sexual differences, and becoming greedy or covetous.

Thus, Hinayana, or "little vehicle" Buddhism, considers this deteriorating cycle to be about 84,000 years in length, to be followed by further cycles of the same length for a grand total of sixty-four cycles. As time moves along, the cycles manifest greater variability. Seven cycles are completed with a destruction by fire, while the eighth is one in which water is the destroyer.

The pattern of seven by fire- one by water is a constant, until the sixty-fourth and final cycle, when wind will take the breath of life away and everything that lives must henceforth reside in the eleven changeless planes above. However, the perishing wind itself perishes, and, after a long period of darkness and chaos, the radiant beings from above again descend to begin anew the cycle of cycles.

Simply getting this straight will tire most western minds to the point of frustration, since it is so very different from the view we commonly hold. Hopefully, it also indicates how space (above and below), time, constancy and variability, vistas and horizons, and planning are woven together in a meaningful pattern where the sense of things is never fully lost but can always be recovered.

The Vedic Hindu Scheme gives more attention to the creation theme, but primarily in terms of eventual recreation, including a kind of pious agnosticism acknowledging that perhaps God himself does not know all that much about the beginnings.[5] For the orthodox Vedic Hindu, the cosmos is eternal but always changes as many different worlds come into existence and pass away.

The personal Brahma (as distinct from Brahma, "the Absolute") has the longest lifespan of any of the gods in the Hindu pantheon. His life lasts some 311,040,000,000,000 years, and his world reaches its end at the conclusion of these trillions of years, only to begin another cycle after a certain period of rest. One of the days in his lifespan consists of a thousand great world periods, and each one of these days is divided into four periods called *yugas*, with each *yuga* consisting of a set of godly years, each of which is equal to about thirty human years. In decreasing order, the fourth *yuga* contains 4800 godly years, the third 3600, with 2400 and 1200 in the second and last *yugas* respectively, for a grand total of 4,320,000 human years.[6]

For Hindus, therefore, everything is involved in enormous periods of time, and their heroes and scriptures come from the unimaginably ancient past. Hence, past time is extremely significant. Constancy and variability are held in balance by a symbol of cyles which occur regularly and yet are always different. The range of involvement is that of the entire cosmos and yet horizons are set with the opening and closing limits of each *yuga*. Like its Buddhist relative, the Hindu scheme holds out the possibility of liberation from the cycle for the individual who attains *nirvana*, but the context in which he does so will never be anything but cyclical.

THE LINEAR

Just as the cyclical view should not be considered exclusively eastern, so the linear should not be simply equated with the western perspective. Although this point of view does indeed prevail in western religion, at least in its "official" teachings, it is always being challenged. Artists like T.S. Eliot and James Joyce made efforts to provide alternative views in the early part of this century, and some recent hippie sub-cultures in the United States have demonstrated considerable enthusiasm for cyclical or spiral-like interpretations of process.

In substance, the linear view signifies a generalization of those views which represent process as irreversible and unidirectional, moving along an imaginary straight line from a genuine beginning to some definitive goal. The Jewish, Christian, and Muslim views are examples of this way of looking at things. Sharing many common sources, they each posit a point of creation which begins the process, and look forward to a final point of either annihilation or transformation. In either case, they envision a totally new state of being, often described as a new heaven and earth. For these traditions the whole process is under the guiding direction of a monotheistically conceived God, who supervises the movement of the process, which, in reality, is "his plan." If the process declines (or stops, as depicted in the latter parts of the aforementioned cycle views) it is described as halting and detoured. The reason for this temporary hesitation in the drive forward is the presence of evil, generally symbolized in terms of the aboriginal Persian model. According to this paradigm, the problem is cosmic. A metaphysical evil spirit is set in unalterable opposition to the good god, creating conflicts between darkness and light, heavenly and earthly realms, until the final struggle when the forces of light will triumph as those of darkness hurtle down into the eternally black and painful regions of loss and punishment.

In this view we find constancy and variability symbolized as the plan of God, and the meanderings of the stream of history caused by the presence of evil. Time's movement is freed of the terror of repetitiousness and is characterized as future-oriented and hope-full. Progress is possible and optimism can be sustained. Spatially, the universe is three-tiered, immortalized in the imagery of Dante and Milton (relying on images from Greece, Rome, and Arabia) with heaven, hell, and earth corresponding to above, below, and in between, each given extremely significant meaning for their inhabitants. Meaning is also dealt with in these views in their depiction of the situation of life as one in which integrity is lost through some originating fault of man, but recaptured or in the process of being recaptured through law, prophecy, and righteous living. The recovery of meaning is variously symbolized, but for Christians nowhere more poignantly than in the interpretation of the Christ-event. One writer, for example, sees in the proclamation of the death and resurrection of Christ, "the surplus of sense over nonsense in history. . . . Being a Christian means detecting the signs of this superabundance in the very order that the human race expresses its own designs."[7]

There are, then, two generalized patterns of religious artistry, shaping man's opinion of the world's processes. The cyclical view represents it as somewhat inexorable, fate-like or indifferent. The linear portrays the movement as one of boundless creativity in which each being and movement contributes to its fullness. Quite naturally, religions teaching one or the other will inculcate quite different attitudes and norms for dealing with the process.

Process as a Functioning Factor in Religious Ethics

The preceding background on some general aspects of process prepares us for considering its function as a factor in religious ethics. This, after all, is the main concern of this chapter, and must now be made as clear as possible. Since the beginning of the book, religious ethics has been likened to a system of two or more parts, aspects, or factors that are functionally related to each other. The generic word "process" has been used to identify one of these factors, and some time was devoted to understanding how religion shapes process elements into a coherent teaching. The task at hand, therefore, is that of demonstrating how these process views are functionally interrelated with the other factors of people and principles in the ethical programs fashioned by religions.

In order to demonstrate this, attention will be first drawn to the way in which the general schemes of cyclical and linear interact with views of man and the guidelines offered for his behavior. Secondly, examples from each of these two general categories will be given, with a major emphasis on the linear view because of its importance in the ethical systems of the west, in which we have been reared.

VERY GENERALLY

The cyclical view of process detailed earlier has a functional interrelationship with the factors of people and principles. This can be seen in the fact that cyclically oriented religions have views of man and recommendations for his behavior which are coherent with their views of process. In its more common interpretations, cyclical world process is not only recurrent, but also has a characteristic decline built into every new universe. This deterioration occurs because of the wickedness of the world's inhabitants who grow increasingly earth-bound in thought and affection, accumulating more and more *karma* weight, which requires rebirth, often in the form of lower level beings such as animals. However, the enlightened holy man, or saint (*arhat*) sees this and strives for release from this endless round, particularly in its punitive aspect. He longs for unity with some absolute like Brahman, Nirvana or the Tao, achieving a cessation of the rebirth cycle, for himself at least. But only the individual can accomplish this, through personal disciplined striving and meditation. He might have the help of a master or guru, but it is generally true to say that the saving community ("church") is less important than the individual in these schemes. The Hindu holy man transcends even caste and caste duty, becoming, in a sense, one who lives beyond the social law. But, the Mahayana Buddhist ideal of a holy man who postpones his release to compassionately assist others offers a definite variant in such generalizations. Yet, it is correct to say that even this *Bodhisattva* is also saved through his own personal efforts, while remaining among his fellow men to aid them in their attainment of individually acquired enlightenment.

Thus, our generalized description of cyclical process is interrelated with a view of man, more individual than social, and ethical principles which enjoin the performance of certain activities leading to both enlightenment and the attainment of liberation from *samsara,* or the endless round of rebirths.

The linear view of process usually depicts life's process as basically good, not inherently tragic, but having become so as a result of some radical derailment in an originating fault of man, a fault which is frequently imitated in the sins of successive generations. Unlike the cyclical view, linear process does not move inevitably through tragic decline to some equally inevitable destruction. Linear process is unidirectional, capable of being set back on the track after a derailment. Animated by this conviction, men look forward to the goal, as to the final ordering of things. But the final order of the day to come is already present in the partial orderings of today, awaiting only its final realization and transformation.

Hence, we find that this view of process has a corresponding view of man in which he is depicted as a collaborator. There is no need to escape or be liberated from a process that is basically good, capable of being redirected and brought to its fulfillment. Man is, therefore, caught up in the process, incapable of escaping it because he cannot escape being intimately linked to other human beings who are also collaborators.

Finally, conjoined with this view of man we find a set of principles particularly appropriate to the linear context of life. Unlike the practices recommended for liberation from endless cycles, linear systems contain advice instructing man in ways and means of setting the process back on its path, and recommend a patient waiting and working for its final consummation. Since man is seen as related to the ultimate, rather than identified with it, his relations carry implications of responsibility. The notions of dependence (creature on creator and redeemed on savior) *both* fit linear process *and* identify man's nature, as well as the rules by which he ought to act. The *hagaddah* or *kerygma* proclaims his situation and relationship, telling the story of what has been done for him by a gracious God who intervenes in history to recover its sense and direction. The *halakha* or *didache* instructs him in responses suited to this divine activity and the relationship it creates, demonstrating how man should behave in order to be thankful as well as to keep his and others' lives moving in the divinely planned direction.

Very generally, then, we can point to a clear correspondence between one's view of process and the related factors of people and principles. This correspondence is no mere accident, but represents a functional relationship, evidenced by the fact that beliefs in one factor are functions of beliefs in the others. While this has been partially demonstrated in a very general way, a fuller demonstration requires that we now turn our attention to the function of the process factor in some specific examples of religious ethics in both the cyclical and linear traditions.

MOST SPECIFICALLY

The cyclical perspective.[8] *Chinese Universism* is a designation originating with J. J. M. de Groot, and refers to the common spiritual foundation of all Chinese conceptions of the world and ethics. It intends to accentuate the fact that the universe, its parts and laws of harmony, are the focal point in most Chinese-based religious traditions. Accordingly, all religious traditions originating in China have a common belief that life is basically a process of bringing about harmony between heaven, earth, and man. They predicate the existence of a harmonious world law (*Tao*) which is variously manifested in life, a law which man must discover and utilize in his efforts to achieve personal and public harmony.

This point of view is strikingly evident in the teachings of Taoism's legendary founder Lao-tzu (seventh century B.C.). It is developed in the Taoist classic the *Tao-Te-Ching* ("The Way and Its Power"), a later work which is attributed to Lao-tzu. This classic elaborates on the general tradition called Chinese Universism and declares that the *Tao* is the basic principle underlying and informing all of the natural world. According to Lao-tzu, the manifestations of *Tao* are seen in the paradoxically effortless yet powerful forces of nature. Water flows downward, to the "humbler" position, yet embodies great energy in its descent. Similarly, water in a lake lies still, but we find it quite unyielding.[9]

From these and similar observations Lao-tzu concluded that the way of the *Tao* is one in which the most beneficial results are achieved by refraining from any activity which would interfere with nature's way. This first law of nature is translated into a primary principle of ethics which promotes non-meddling activity as the way of the Tao, and is extolled as the principal responsibility of the man who would effectively cooperate with the harmonization process at work in the universe.

Chuang-tzu, a more philosophically and mystically inclined Taoist of the fourth century B.C., added another dimension to the process view contained in the *Tao-Te-Ching*. Earlier in this chapter we noted some elements which constitute process views, and included among them "time and space, vistas and horizons." In these terms we can identify something which Chuang-tzu mused about and, in his musing, added to the Taoist interpretation of world process.

Chuang-tzu arrived at the conclusion that life was limited, while knowledge was not so. The finite character of the world and human life made itself felt and was one of the points of dispute between scholars. In the terms used earlier in this chapter, they were trying to decide what to say about time and space, and what limits were imposed upon their vistas by the horizons they could see. Chuang-tzu thought he had broken through this problem by noting that life is limited, and knowledge unlimited, but that we ought to ignore the passing of time and find pleasure in the realm of the infinite (without limitation).[10]

Accordingly, harmony, or the way of the *Tao*, is to be achieved, in Chuang-tzu's philosophy, by the true man who understands life's deceptions and lives in the underlying unity of life, a unity in which there can be no change because this man truly achieves an immortal identification with the infinite. As you can see, this treatment is considerably more nuanced than that attributed to Lao-tzu, and you may find it significant that Chuang-tzu also arrived at a more nuanced interpretation of man and the sage, which will be considered in some detail in the following chapter.

The Chinese tradition begun by Master K'ung, and called Confucianism, shares the same spiritual heritage of Universist thinking which animated the Taoist tradition. However, this heritage took a different turn in the work of Confucius, born near the end of Lao-tzu's life. It is quite popular to point out the diametrically opposed political principles of Taoism and Confucianism, usually depicted as proponents of anarchy and reform through education, respectively. It is equally popular to note the differences between the human ideal proposed by these traditions, associating the ideal of the sage with Taoism, and that of the aristocrat-scholar with Confucianism. What is not frequently mentioned, however, is the differences in their view of world process, as specified in what we have been calling the constituent element of "time."

The flux of time is acknowledged in both the Taoist and Confucian traditions. Chuang-tzu grappled with it in some of his work and resolved the problem by encouraging man to attain a timeless wisdom which extricated him from the flux. In Confucianism, however, the tradition and heritage from the past is so prominent that it seems to head most Confucian thinkers into a past-oriented frame of mind. The preoccupation with ancestors, elders, and the inherited traditions of social and political custom seems to have led inevitably in this direction.

Confucius saw himself as a transmitter of the wisdom of the past, rather than a creator of new understandings (*Analects* VII.1).[11] He looked back upon the era of the Chou kings as the ideal time of feudal peace and order, and idealized it as something of a golden age which the Chinese should try to imitate in the socio-political disarray of his time. However, this love of the past was not something independent of the *Tao*. Confucius held fast to the Universist belief in a natural order, with his own special understanding of the *Tao* ("Heaven" in the Confucian tradition). He conceived of Heaven as a personal guiding force in life, expressing a will which was binding upon man. The emphasis on the past and the historical was simply Confucius' way of determining what Heaven wanted, for he believed that the traditions, customs and literature of the past made this clearer than anything else.[12]

The fourth-century Confucian, Mencius, followed suit, but modified the tradition somewhat, emphasizing as he did a past "age of innocence" in each individual. The past had to be recovered or imitated, but the most significant past for Mencius was that time in each one of our lives which he identified as the time of the child-like heart.[13]

In the following century, Hsün-Tzu broke the continuity of past-oriented Confucian process thinking by putting forth a hard-headed realism strongly disillusioned with the old-order ideal. With states collapsing all around him, he found no comfort in the traditional Confucian hope for re-establishing the old ideal order, and tried to rework the element of time in the Confucian view, attempting to shorten the gap between the past and the present by emphasizing the present, which could contain the past within it if people would only regulate their affairs. In addition to this modification, Hsün-tzu also reworked the personalistic interpretation of Heaven, replacing it with a view of life's process that is described as rational and naturalistic, if not in fact mechanical. The point he thought essential was the recognition of the fact that life's process of *Tao* worked independently of man's activities. He concluded, therefore, that efforts made to understand Heaven were utterly useless. Speculating about Heaven and neglecting human effort was largely a waste of time, for men ought rather spend themselves in harnessing, exploiting, controlling and regulating the powers in life.[14]

From these few examples we can see that the traditional Chinese view of world process was most prominent in the intellectual ferment occurring in the first few centuries of Taoism and Confucianism. It is also interesting to note the correlation between the stands taken on process and those taken on the meaning of people and principles. We shall elaborate on this point in the following pages, but call your attention to it now in order to encourage thinking in terms of the functional interrelationships of the key factors in the Chinese systems of religious ethics.

Hinduism-Buddhism.   Our next set of examples comes from Hinduism and the Buddhism which arose in protest against certain emphases in the priest-controlled teachings of Brahmanic Hinduism in the sixth century B.C.

We should first note that Hinduism and Buddhism, like all Indian-based religions, are in general agreement about the cyclical nature of world process.

And, while Buddhism placed more emphasis on the degree of suffering immanent in life, they both agree on the possibility of a saving existence called *nirvana*. From the ethical point of view, their principal differences are found in what they consider appropriate ways to reach this salvation.

Secondly, we can illustrate these differences of opinion in what the *Bhagavad Gita* outlines as the three ways to salvation: (1) *Karma Marga*, the Way of Action (2) *Jnana Marga*, the Way of Insight, and (3) *Bhakti Marga*, the Way of Devotion.[15] As we study these differences we will be particularly concerned with identifying the process factor and its interactions with the other factors. Hence, we will limit ourselves to a mention of just those historical facts which make these points clear.

(1) *Karma Marga* is a very old way, emphasizing action, duty, domestic ritual. It was defined during the period when the sacred writings called *Brahmanas* were being added to the older *Vedas*, that is between the ninth and seventh centuries B.C. Furthermore, *karma marga* was stabilized precisely when the caste system was getting settled, toward the end of the seventh century. This *karma* line of ethical teaching was controlled by the highest of the castes, the Brahmin priests, and set them to thinking out codes of law which reinforced the caste system, detailing caste duties and culminating in the famous *Code of Manu* by 200 B.C.

The *Code of Manu* gave detailed prescriptions for household sacramental rites, caste duties, social and dietary laws, authoritatively describing the works required for salvation according to the way of action, and assumed the Vedic view of cyclical process mentioned earlier in this chapter.

(2) *Jnana Marga* emerged between the seventh and fourth centuries, B.C., emphasizing the inward activity of mind and spirit in opposition to older Aryan ideals of teachers, warriors, and husbandmen. Ascetics and philosophical thinkers increased during this period, which saw the birth of the Jainist and Buddhist ideals. These latter, along with the Hindu *Upanishads*, emphasized knowledge (Jainist omniscience and Buddhist enlightenment) as the truest path to salvation.

The principal change worked in the older views of process was the addition of an emphasis on rebirth and reincarnation. During this period caste limitations were deemphasized since the rebirth element in the process factor pointed up the possibility of being reborn into different castes as punishment or reward along the path of attaining liberation by insight.

(3) *Bhakti Marga* represents the most dramatic change in the Hindu-Buddhist process factor, and clearly demonstrates the functional interrelationship of the three factors in a religious ethic of the cyclical variety. The emphasis on piety and devotion so central to *bhakti* is but intimated in the *Code of Manu*. But, while Manu was giving his code its final form, devotional literature such as the *Bhagavad Gita* was increasing. From the fourth century B.C., to the fourth century A.D., Indian thought, especially in the north, began to emphasize ardent and hopeful devotion in an effort to satisfy the

needs of ordinary people who were by and large not capable of the intro-spection and reflection idealized in *jnana*.

At precisely the time when Buddhism was beginning to take hold in China, north Indian Buddhists were developing the classics of devotional Buddhism. By the third century A.D., they had fixed the ideal of *bhakti marga* in two writings known as the *Pure Land Sutras* and the *Lotus of the Wonderful Law*. From the third to the fifth centuries this devotionalism caught on in China, and appealed to the broad masses of people. In China it carries the name *Ching-t'u* (*Jodo* in Japan), and sometimes is also called Mahayana Buddhism.[16]

The prospect opened up by these scriptures was a most happy one. It portrayed a land of lakes and flowers, music and rare delights. There, the Buddha of immeasureable light lived in perfect peace with numberless human and superhuman beings. And this paradise was open to anyone who had but the slightest devotion, or who would call on the Buddha to extend them his merciful compassion.

From this point of view Mahayana, or "Large-Vehicle" Buddhism was a most apt designation, offering as it did a gospel of new hope and confidence to wide ranges of people who were unable to pursue the saving path of *jnana marga* as idealized in the ascetic monk.

What is of particular interest here is the change and reverberations worked by the process factor in this Indian-based Buddhist tradition. As we saw in both *karma* and *jnana marga*, the process view remained fairly steady when Hindus and Buddhists shifted emphases from social activity to mental discipline. However, when devotionalism became popular, the shape of the salvation goal became more picturesque and emotionally appealing.

In conjunction with this change in the process factor, there were also changes in the people and principles factors. The ideal of a compassionate *bodhisattva* replaced the austere and ascetical *arhat*. Principles gave more emphasis to loving devotion to the Buddha and concern for others as compared to the rigorous intellectual pursuit of personal self-discipline and enlightenment.

The shifts of interpretation taking place in the people and principles factors will be noted again in the following chapters. At this point we should underscore the turn taken by the view of process. We should be able to see two things from the brief sketch given here. First of all, the Hindu-Buddhist process notions change as they move from *karma* to *bhakti marga*. Process becomes more picturesque in its description of the goal, and more devotional in the context in which this goal is attained. Secondly, there are correlative and functionally related changes occurring in the views of man and the guidelines suggested for his behavior.

Before we conclude our considerations of the Indian views of process, we should call attention to some of the most picturesque of the devotional literature, namely the *Puranas*. Developed in the first to fourth centuries

A.D., during the strong emphasis on devotionalism, they provide an extremely interesting sample of Hindu artistry in dealing with spatial elements in the interpretation of world process. They paint a picture of the universe as a place where gods and men interact, accentuating the roles of Vishnu and Shiva in their dealings with men. As a result of these interactions, certain places are identified as sacred, the memorialized locations of great events involving the gods. The Himalayas and the Ganges are two such places to which they attach a religious significance. Through the *Puranas* and the thought stimulated by them, the Hindu tradition can be said to have developed a "sacred geography," a way of interpreting the spatial element that designates certain locations in the theater of human activity as holy places.[17]

The linear perspective. This view of world process is primarily western, recognizable as the one most of us have been taught, and the source of considerable discussion in the last few decades. The linear view of process, taken as a generalization composed of several slightly variant interpretations, has had the allegiance of numerous adherents from different cultural backgrounds over a long period of time. We can identify, for example, the Jewish linear views of history, those of Zoroastrianism, and the Muslim and Christian models of linear process.

Of these, the Jewish is, perhaps, the most ancient, and the originating viewpoint for both the Christian and Muslim interpretations. However, knowing the long-standing opposition to philosophical analysis of its faith, we might doubt the validity of a "systems approach" to Jewish ethics in particular. Except for a few traces of rational argument in the Bible, an occasional use of logic in rabbinical expositions of the Torah, and a flirtation with Hellenistic thought in the first century before Christ, the first two thousand years of Judaism have been rather consciously anti-systematic. Even the last thousand years have witnessed only sporadic efforts at systematic philosophizing, notably in the medieval period and during that of the enlightenment. Therefore, one might legitimately question the validity of viewing Jewish ethics in the light of a systems analogy. Recall if you will, that a systems approach posits *only* that certain factors in all ethical systems are in fact functionally interrelated, *not* that their proponents consciously and systematically attempt to keep them such. Thus, even where ethicians disclaim efforts at rational consistency, there may be a systematic coherence of which they merely do not wish to speak.

On this premise one could go back through the various stages of teaching in the *Tanakh* (Jewish "Bible") and demonstrate the coherence between the Jewish view of eschatology and the kind of law they used to instruct the faithful in those times. Pre-exilic views of process have corresponding principles different in both kind and quantity from those taught in the levitical code which operates on the later modified view of process, one shaken and purified by the harsh experience of the exile.

However, lest this presentation appear to force a typology on Judaic ethics, or press it into categories unduly restrictive to its real character, it seems wiser to take some examples of Jewish thought from a time when they are, of their own admission, more consciously philosophical. Hence, the following examples come from nineteenth and twentieth century Jewish philosophers and theologians who acknowledge that social emancipation of the Jews has thrust upon them both the obligation and opportunity of analyzing their faith rationally.

Jewish Ethics since Kant.[18]   We can distinguish at least four strains of a more admittedly philosophical Jewish theology since the time of Immanuel Kant.

The first reconstructs and revises the Kantian emphasis on the primacy of ethics. It is rooted in the work of both Hermann Cohen and Leo Baeck, who, in different ways, analyze the relationship between law and monotheism in the Jewish faith.

The second school, under the leadership of Mordecai Kaplan, explores the possibilities of understanding Judaism from the naturalist and nationalist points of view.

The first two positions bear more pointedly on the issues to be treated in Chapters III and IV. Hence, extended comment on them will be reserved until that point in our study. But, the third and fourth strains, namely, those of religious existentialism inspired by Martin Buber, and neo-orthodoxy led by Abraham Heschel, are most relevant to a discussion of how the process factor functionally affects other factors in Jewish ethics, and will, therefore, be dealt with in this present chapter.

Buber gave us the most complete picture of his theology in his 1923 publication *I and Thou*, written in the post World-War I context of the death of older value systems and the search for new ones. For Buber, life's process is symbolized in the all-embracing totality of an originating relational event, in which the *I and Thou* relationship between God and His People is established. This covenant event, of which Sinai is the paradigm, gives us our fundamental picture of life's personal, social, and cosmic situations. All problems, both theoretical and practical, are seen only as parts segregated from this larger whole, and retain their significance only by preserving this vital connection. Ethics, then, is in a context of an originating relationship, and principles of action are meaningless if they do not relate functionally to the primoridal process factor.

In an extraordinarily creative manner Buber re-created the teachings and legends of the 18th through 19th century East European tradition of Hasidic communal mysticism. With exceptional artistry, he refashioned an interpretation of the relations of man to God that keeps man intimately involved with his fellow men and his world, with no apparent need to turn away from them. The originating relational event is not a mere date in the past to be commemorated and thereby related to. On the contrary, it is eternally present, related to mystically, not, however, apart from men and the world, but precisely in and through them. Thus, Buber's ethical principles recommend an active and realistic mysticism, in which man can be related to the divine only through the human in community with others. In summary, the process is what God is doing with man in dialogue, and the principles accordingly counsel us to see this and cooperate with it in the fully concrete here and now.[19]

The fourth, and neo-orthodox strain of reflective Jewish theology since the time of Kant, is guided by the towering figure of *Abraham Joshua Heschel*. This professor of Jewish Ethics and Mysticism at New York's Jewish Theological Seminary has devoted much of his life elaborating a theology of the *pathos* of God. It was set down most forcefully in his book on the prophets, from which the following quotation, most pertinent to this particular study, is taken:

> The universe is done. The greater masterpiece still undone, still in the process of being created, is history. For accomplishing His grand design, God needs the help of man. Man is and has the instrument of God, which he may or may not use in consonance with the grand design. Life is clay, and righteousness the mold in which God wants history to be shaped. But human beings, instead of fashioning the clay, deform the shape.
>
> The world is full of iniquity, of injustice and idolatry. The people offer animals; the priests offer incense. But God needs mercy, righteousness; His needs cannot be satisfied in the temples, in space, but only in history, in time. It is within the realm of history that man is charged with God's mission.*

The context in which he says this is one where he asks, rhetorically, "Why should religion, the essence of which is the worship of God, put such stress on justice for man?"† The answer, of course, is that righteousness (justice and mercy) is not merely a value or virtue; it's what life is all about. It is, in fact, God's part in human life, his stake in human life, his "stake in human history."‡ One can readily see manifested here a strong preference for the process symbols of the prophets, and a direction offered for principle-making that will be heavily freighted with the same prophetic *pathos*. The effort to attain justice in human life is no trifling matter in this ethic, no mere human responsibility for which man "answers" to God after death. God "lives or dies" in an ethic that builds its requirements on a view

---

* Abraham Heschel, *The Prophets* (New York: Harper & Row, Publishers, 1962), p. 198.

† *ibid.*

‡ *ibid.*

of God as caught in man's predicament, as a result of His having determined to become involved in human history.[20]

Everything Heschel writes bears the imprint of the presence of this transcendental demand; God has acted in a certain fashion and given a law that demands our obedience. This can be seen in a collection of essays and lectures entitled *The Insecurity of Freedom*,[21] in which he ranges over the passionate concerns of a Jewish believer living in the America of today. The racial conflict as well as Jewish education, the trivialization life of in America as well as the Christian ecumenical movement come under his scrutiny. Each treatment, however, bears the stamp of the prophetic theology of *pathos* and demonstrates how Judaism's view of life's process shapes its ethical principles.

> The most commanding idea that Judaism dares to think is that freedom, not necessity, is the source of all being. The universe was not caused, but created. Behind mind and matter, order and relations, the freedom of God obtains. The inevitable is not eternal. All compulsion is a result of choice. A tinge of that exemption from necessity is hiding in the folds of the human spirit.*
>
> Judaism is forever engaged in a bitter battle against man's deeply rooted belief in fatalism and its ensuing inertia in social, moral, and spiritual conditions. Abraham started in rebellion against his father and the gods of his time. His great distinction was not in being loyal and conforming, but in defying and initiating.*

With a becoming sophistication Heschel here outlines a very fundamentalist theology, one which demonstrates how his view of the universe and its process sets up a corresponding set of principles. Freedom, for Heschel, is not exhausted when we have simply spoken of psychological freedom of deliberation and decision. It further implies being open and responsive to transcendence. Only in this way can man be responsible, and avert the humdrum standardizing that diminishes his value and saps his desire to strive for greater justice.[22]

Post-reformation Christian ethics. Christianity is another widely known example of a religious tradition built on a linear view of world process. Its ethical principles have become so well known in the West that they are frequently discussed in isolation from other intimately related tenets.

As a result, many of these discussions have taken place on the basis of incomplete clues. Debates, such as the so-called new morality or situation ethics disputes of the sixties, were often hampered by a failure to see the connections prevailing between process, people, and principles.

---

* Abraham Heschel, *The Insecurity of Freedom* (New York: Farrar, Straus & Giroux, Inc., 1966), Copyright (c) 1966, pp. 13, 14.

The following quotation from James Gustafson makes the same point in different terminology:

> The way in which the debate has attended to the moral level of discourse without sufficiently moving to other levels is in part responsible for its being misplaced. It has tended to assume that the matter of how moral decisions are made could be separated from other considerations. I hope it is now clear that if one chooses to argue against "contextualism" one has to direct his argument to the theological and ethical reasons given for the stress on context. Thus against Barth, Lehmann, and Sittler, one's argument ought primarily to be a theological argument. *It is because these men have a certain view of God and his activity that they find contextualism congenial as an approach to ethics.* None of them is fixed upon the question 'How do men decide what to do?' as if this ethical question were capable of abstraction from fundamental theological convictions in the strict sense. If one chooses to argue against H. R. Niebuhr, one would have to argue not only on theological grounds (not explicated in this essay), *but also on the grounds of a moral anthropology. Is man to be understood as responder and answerer, or is he better understood as maker and citizen?* If one chooses to argue against the demand for refined social analysis of the context of action, the character of one's concerns might be directed to whether the context is properly understood through the means of social research, and whether such a proposal does not carry with it unexplicated ethical and theological assumptions.
>
> Similarly, if one argues against principles, one has to be particular about certain questions. *From what sources are the principles derived? From nature, or from biblical revelation, or from the ethos of the Christian community? How are the principles used?* For giving direction to goals, or for the determination of right conduct? As prescriptive principles, or as analytical and illuminating principles?*

Gustafson's article, labelling some of these debates as misplaced, demonstrates that you cannot thread your way through the "context versus principles" discussion without reaching back into the assumptions of a theologian or that of his tradition to discover the underlying interpretations they hold about man and the process in which he is involved.

We find an intimate connection between the principles and process views of several of the recent debaters on the American scene. Joseph Fletcher sizes up the process as that of the Einsteinian world of relativity, and, hence, his ethical principles recommend situational decision making.[23]

---

* James M. Gustafson, "Context vs. Principles: A Misplaced Debate," in *New Theology* #3 (New York: The Macmillan Company, 1966), p.99. By permission of the Harvard Theological Review. (Note: Italics mine.)

Paul Lehmann recommends that we try to make human life more human because he is convinced that this is the basic meaning of the process in which we are involved. God's own activity, he notes, is that of making human life more human, and Christians become alert to, moved by, and skillful in interpreting the requirements of this process within the context of the church community (*koinonia*).[24] Some Roman Catholics, such as Bernard Haring and Charles Curran, have taken part in the larger debate in occasional time-outs from the internal struggles of a legalistic catholic ethic in the process of being reformed. They suggest that man ought to say yes to the call given to follow Christ, and that man surrender himself to this Christ who can transform him, implanting His "Law" in a person's heart by the power of the spirit. For Haring and Curran, then, call and discipleship, gift and sanctification are the dominant symbols of the process, and create the necessity of talking about principles in terms of "response-ability."[25]

The process-principles connections are fairly obvious in the debaters just mentioned. Yet, one of them, J. Fletcher, would certainly want to deny any systematic connection between these two factors. His writings demonstrate a strong preference for light banter about the connections between the new situational rules and their presuppositions in certain philosophical and theological assumptions. Dealing with this matter only in passing, as he threads his way through cases and casualties in contemporary morality, he occasionally makes statements like the following: "In ethics as in physics we have left behind the Newtonian world for the Einsteinian world; not mechanics now but dynamics."[26] Furthermore, he admittedly agrees with G. F. Woods that faith and ethics are basically unrelated, that the attempt to establish the autonomy of moral principles is valid and largely successful, except for a few pockets of resistance from the defenders of natural theology.[27] Logically, then, there should be no functional relationship between things believed and moral rules, but Fletcher clearly defies such logic noting time and again that love is the only rule—*because* Jesus' summary of the law and the prophets is "an absolute and universally valid imperative."[28] It would seem that there must be some connection between Jesus and the command accepted from him; something about him must be believed if a man is to take orders from him; belief and moral rules must be related. In fact, to logically hold Fletcher's position Jesus would have to have some kind of central role in the whole process of life, and would have to be a certain kind of person with a special relation to people to be able to claim authority demanding obedience.

It would appear that there are some hidden assumptions in Fletcher's position. He has, in fact, been criticized on just these grounds, and has reacted unfavorably protesting that assumption-talk is largely absurd anyway, while rule-talk without assumptions makes all the sense in the world.[29] This cannot, however, be supported by simply turning the designations medieval, metaphysical, and metaethical into swear words, as Fletcher does.[30] Despite his protests, the assumptions and metaphysical statements about man and process can readily be found in his own writings. For example, he states that man is finite, imperfect, and a *creature*.[31] The latter term is clearly not something that can be verified on purely empirical grounds, and must be a matter of belief, a view of man held true with the certitude of metaphysical or theological faith. And, like it or not, it is a metaethical statement, if only in disguise, saying that man *is* a certain kind of being, and going on to use it as a presupposition in making recommendations about decision-making.

It would seem that Fletcher does have some definite views on process, people and principles which interact, albeit unconsciously, in his ethical statements. To make them more conscious may, in his mind, share the same pejorative connotation as "hellenization" and "medievalization," as if the error-making capacity of man ground to a halt centuries ago. However, by taking the issue out of the realm of terms used in ontology, and placing it in the language of process-people-principles, as does this study, he may be able to agree that the first two factors do have some connection to what he says about the third factor in isolation from the others.

In sharp contrast to Fletcher is the work of Harvey Cox, who has evidenced both an interest and a skill in working out the connections between different factors in Christian teaching. Much of his interest in recent years has been a search for a new evangelism, for relevance for the christian gospel in the secular city,[32] and achieving an "adequate perspective for a politics of the future"[33] acknowledging the fact that our century's preoccupation with the future is a colossal challenge to traditional Christianity.

Consistent with this interest, he singles out three predominant perspectives from which Christians have traditionally forged their principles of responsibility for the world. He calls these the *apocalyptic* or falling-firmament perspective, the *teleological* or sprouting-spore process, and the *prophetic* or the perspective of unconditioned possibility. In the following quotation he demonstrates the functional relationship between these views of process and the kind of principles that come from proponents of these variant interpretations.

> In contrast to apocalyptic, the prophetic mood has confidence in the worth of moral and political action. It visualizes the future of this world not as an inferno that ushers in some other world but as the only world we have and the one that man is unavoidably summoned to shape in accord with his hopes and memories. The prophetic mentality rejects the apocalyptic notion that this or that elect group can escape cosmic ruination or is destined to rule the rest of us. It sees people inextricably intertwined in the future of the world.
>
> Against the teleological view, the prophetic sees the *eschata* (future) transforming the *arche* (past) rather than vice versa. It sees

the future with its manifold possibilities undoing the determinative grip of the past, of the beginning. In contrast to most forms of teleology, prophecy defines man as principally historical rather than as natural. Without denying his kinship to the beasts, it insists that his freedom to hope and remember, his capacity to take responsibility for the future is not an accident but defines his nature.

But most important, prophecy sees everything in the light of its possibilities for human use and celebration. Without rejecting the influence of historical continuities, it insists that our interest in history, if it is not merely antiquarian, arises from our orientation toward the future. The Israelite prophets called the past to memory not to divinize it but to remind people that the God of the covenant still expected things from them in the future.*

This quotation from Cox is an excellent illustration of the kind of concerns troubling Christian ethicians in a world where the possibilities of "going sour" loom ever larger. Throughout the new morality debate theologians had been concerned with the need to fashion treatises *On Being Responsible*,[34] and to suit ethical guidelines to a situation defined as a "world come of age."[35] They became convinced that, to take but one example, God will not take care of our need for water without man's responsible steps to ensure its continued and unpolluted supply. Reinterpretations of process provoked changes in the principles offered as guidelines, and theologians like Cox were of service in pointing out the systematic relationship between the two. In doing so, Cox, and others, provided students of religious ethics an opportunity of seeing how coherency operates as a criterion in ethical systems, requiring that what is put forth as a process symbol be functionally interrelated with what is recommended in behavioral guidelines.

In the treatment of Christian ethics so far we have considered only a few samples of contemporary American spokesmen and some of their differences of opinion. In these samplings we can find ample evidence of the fact that views about process have functional ties with the principles suggested by their proponents.

The examples chosen do, however, point up the fact that we find a wide diversity of opinion embraced under the general name of Christian. They demonstrate how difficult it is to make any generalizations about Christian ethics, and prompt us to be most precise in defining the goals of our study.

In this and following chapters we are trying to identify the factors in some of the principal systems of Christian ethics, and demonstrate the functional interactions between these factors. This chapter focuses on the process factor, the interpretations Christians give to what's happening in the world, and how Christian principles are shaped in conformity with these

---

* Harvey Cox, "Tradition and the Future, II," in *Christianity and Crisis*, **27**: 17 (October 16, 1967), p. 230.

views. But, as the examples demonstrate, there are several such views going under the name of Christian. They could possibly be divided according to the denominations holding them, but that is often misleading, if not partisan. They can also be considered in terms of their preferences for one or more of the common Christian symbols emphasizing particular aspects of the world process. Even within one particular denomination we will find a diversity of emphases on the meaning of process, and hence a diversity of ethical teachings. Cox brought this out in noting the differences between theologies emphasizing the apocalyptic, teleological, or prophetic view of process. In systems language, we could say that the varied output of any Christian community is due to a variety of inputs, some of which come from the various emphases on process that are fed into the denominational system.

Thus, both for the sake of clarity and to maintain the viewpoint of the detached-within, we should characterize systems of Christian ethics in some terms other than merely sectarian ones. We can, for instance, identify four dominant strains of Christian ethics since the time of the Protestant Reformation in the sixteenth century. We can designate them in terms of their preferred symbol of linear process. This will not necessarily tell us which denomination prefers this symbol, but will simply provide a convenient way of talking about the wide diversity of ethical systems prevailing within the generalized linear tradition of Christianity.

In explaining what does and should happen along the straight line of history, Christians have, at least since the Reformation, preferred one of the following four symbols of process:

1. The Creation-Fall-Redemption Symbol*
2. The Justification Symbol
3. The Sanctification Symbol
4. The Discipleship Symbol

The interpretations common to the *creation-fall-redemption* grouping show a marked preference for the belief that "God acts and man reacts." According to this view of process the context of our activity is a historical datum from the past, not something to be arranged as time unfolds, but something which simply needs to be made manifest. And such a manifestation is seen in the Christ and the Biblical Word. Through them man can know both who he is, and that his relationship to God is one of dependence requiring obedient service. Thus, man should give his first loyalty to God's commands, looking with suspicion on all other guidelines for human behavior.

Even within this single grouping preferring the creation-fall-redemption symbol, there exist a considerable variety of positions, depending on how you understand the nature of man's dependence, the meaning of revelation, and the relative importance attached to some particular commandments

* Cf. Appendix.

of God. Nonetheless, all post-Reformation ethics resting on this symbol of process inevitably adopt views of man and behavioral principles which correspond with the process factor.

Those who prefer the *justification* symbol as the chief sign of what is happening in life have a great deal to say about what happens to the man who is "justified." They explain this happening as something worked by God, who transcends man, declares him guilty of sin, and justifies him by no longer holding him to his debt. This divine activity is largely interpreted as extrinsic to man, the action of a sovereign just God who is also merciful and forgiving.

The interpretations common to those preferring the *sanctification* symbol focus more attention on man (the people factor), but necessarily must also say something about process. What they emphasize is the condition of the world as one that needs to be transformed, and that man is the key to that transforming process. But the process of transformation is a divine activity, working on man through Christ's saving Spirit. The world, in this view, is being made holy because God is working on man, sanctifying him, and through him the rest of creation.

We have called the last general grouping of post-Reformation Christian process symbols the *discipleship* category. With this term we intend to signify one strain of Christian ethics which prefers to answer questions about process in terms of the following or imitation of Christ. While systems using this process symbol rely heavily on teachings about Jesus as the perfect man, and emphasize his principles as the best possible, they also identify what can be called a process factor which is intimately linked to the other two. In simple terms the process is described as following in the footsteps of the Master, or defined as some type of conversion process in which the disciple begins to take on the patterns of behavior proper to Jesus Christ.

The fuller implications of the factors in these four categories of process symbols will become clearer as we move through the next two chapters. For the present, our principal concern is to note them, and to partially demonstrate how these views of process are implied and functionally operative in four general categories of Christian ethics since the sixteenth century. And some of the contemporary U. S. theologians mentioned in this chapter give evidence of this functional relationship in their work. Whether consciously or not, Fletcher's process symbol seems to be that of discipleship, functionally related to the rule of love which demands absolute obedience to at least the summary command of Jesus. Bernard Haring and Charles Curran are examples of theologians who hold something of a sanctification view of world process and promote Christian principles which recommend surrender to Christ's transforming activity through his spirit. Paul Lehmann's position contains elements of both the creation-fall-redemption process symbol and that of justification, emphasizing as he does the primacy of God's activity and the corresponding principles which advise Christians to become aware of and skillful in the interpretation of this divine activity in the context of a Christian community.

The Muslim religious ethic.   Islam is another, and our last, example of a major world religion whose linear view of process is functionally related to its views of people and principles. The choice of a specific Muslim example is, however, something of a problem, since Islam has generally valued a high diversity of opinion and emphasized the equality of all believers. There has never been an authoritative clergy, caste of priests, or sacrosanct body of wise men, with a monopoly on understanding Muslim religious ethics. Hence, almost any example, such as the one proposed here, will be open to question and debate. But the sample I propose is one with some advantages since it comes from literature written for the Muslim Students Association of the United States and Canada.

The eighth unit of the Muslim Student Correspondence Course is entitled "Moral Teachings of Islam," and in its first two pages makes mention of the process factor. It notes that Islamic morality rests on the foundation of an *active* faith, by which one fulfills his obligations to God and man, working for the establishment of God's law across the earth. In faith built on the Qu'ran, the Muslim must affirm the world, but should see it and his life as in the process of preparing for the Day of Judgment.[36]

The Muslim's understanding of himself and his obligations will be given more attention in the following chapters, but we must at least note here that the process factor is extremely influential in all Muslim systems of ethics. For the Muslim, world process implies more than just working one's way to judgment day. It is also imbued with the implications of *tawhid* (the unity of transcendent being-Allah). *Tawhid* establishes the transcendence of Allah, the unity of all men in relationship to him, and sees him as the Creator and Sustainer, whose will is to be actualized in time and space.[37] The significance of this belief can be seen in the fact that, if the Muslim is to understand himself and his moral obligations, he must take this interpretation of process seriously. He must be able to see the whole of his life as submitting to and actualizing the will of Allah in all of his activities, as well as those of social and political institutions. Without this view of life's process and context, any views about man and his behavior are simply incomplete. Hence, we can say, in the language of this text, that the process factor in our Muslim example is functionally inter-related with the people and principles factors.

STUDY QUESTIONS

1. Is the Marxist theory of history cyclical or linear? Is it in part religious, that is, containing an implicit linear messianism?

2. Are all cyclical views of world process necessarily pessimistic and fatalistic?

3. Apply Howard Warshaw's comments about general fictions contained in the art of advertising to some popular television commerical.

4. Take one of Herman Hesse's novels, such as *Siddartha*, and try to identify its process factor(s) as either cyclical or linear.

5. Trace the changes in the Confucian view of process, or "heaven," from Confucius, through Mencius, to Hsün-tzu.

6. Try to either verify or disprove the contention that the Judaeo-Christian creation myth supports a nature-despoiling technology.[38] Can you give any examples of the functional interactions of creation views with western principles-plans-procedures?

7. Do you think it accurate to say that the God of mainline Christian churches in America is most at home in the past? What tensions would be placed on their traditional ethical principles if they moved toward process views like that contained in the "theology of hope?"[39]

8. Consider some sample of "new left" views of revolution and history.[40] Try to determine if it is cyclical or linear, and try to demonstrate the functional ties between it and the statements and strategies of its proponents.

NOTES

1. Albert Camus, *The Rebel*, trans. Anthony Bower (New York: Vintage, 1956), p. 252.

2. William A. Clebsch, *From Sacred to Profane America: The Role of Religion in American History* (New York: Harper & Row, Publishers, 1968).

3. Camus, *The Rebel*, p. 259.

4. Cf. the "Dialogues of Buddha", as interpreted by Winston L. King, in *Introduction to Religion* (New York: Harper & Row, Publishers, 1968), pp. 190–94.

5. Cf. *Rig-Veda* X. 129 as found in *The Great Asian Religions: An Anthology* (New York: The Macmillan Company, 1969), p. 21, #7.

6. Cf. Helmuth Von Glasenapp, *Non-Christian Religions A to Z* (New York: Grosset and Dunlap, 1963), pp. 113–17, Cf. also *Vishnu Purana* VI: 1 and IV: 24, trans. H. H. Wilson (London: John Murray, 1840), pp. 621, 482–84.

7. Attributed to Paul Ricoeur, with no cross reference, in *New Theology* No. 5, ed. Marty-Peerman (New York: The Macmillan Company, 1968), p. 11.

8. Much of the factual data in this section on the cyclical perspective comes from Von Glasenapp, *op. cit.*, pp. 24 ff., 52 ff., and Ninian Smart, *The Religious Experience of Mankind* (New York: Charles Scribner's Sons, 1968), pp. 97 ff., 141 ff.

9. Cf. *Sources of Chinese Tradition*, Vol. I, compiled by W. T. de Bary, Wing-Tsit-Chan, and Burton Watson (New York: Columbia University Press, 1960), #8, p. 53; #78, p. 61.

10. *op. cit.*, p. 73.

11. *op. cit.*, p. 20.

12. *op. cit.*, p. 17.

13. *op. cit.*, p. 88.

14. Cf. *Hsün Tzu (Basic Writings)*, trans. by Burton Watson (New York: Columbia University Press, 1963), section 17, pp. 79–88. Cf. also *Sources of Chinese Tradition*, Vol. I, pp. 103–4.

15. The threefold division of the ways of salvation comes from the *Bhagavad Gita* III, VI, XI, as cited in Ainslie T. Embree, *The Hindu Tradition* (New York: Modern Library, Inc., 1966), pp. 122–28. Note: as used in this text it does not intend to imply, as does the *Gita*, that the third way (*bhakti*) is the truest way. Rather, we use the same terms as those in the *Gita* to give a reasonably clear distinction between the different ideals occurring throughout the history of Hinduism-Buddhism.

16. With the advent of Mahayana ("Greater-Vehicle") Buddhism, the older form of Buddhism was pejoratively termed Hinayana ("Little-Vehicle") by the newcomers to designate older Buddhism's exclusiveness (limited to monks and incapable of "carrying as many passengers as the newer variety"). Hence, some prefer the less abusive term Theravadan Buddhism, although it is a later designation given to the more traditional Buddhism as it is presently found in Ceylon, Burma, and parts of Southeast Asia.

17. Cf. Embree, *The Hindu Tradition*, p. 220.

18. What follows on Jewish ethics relies in part on the work of Eugene Borowitz, *A New Jewish Theology in the Making* (Philadelphia: The Westminster Press, 1968), esp. pp. 71 ff., and on Nathan Rotenstreich's *Jewish Philosophy in Modern Times* (New York: Holt, Rinehart and Winston, Inc., 1968).

19. Martin Buber, *I and Thou*, trans. Ronald Gregor Smith, 2nd ed. (New York: Charles Scribner's Sons, 1958); _____, *Hasidism and Modern Man*, trans. with an introduction by Maurice Friedman (New York: Harper & Row, Publishers, 1966); and M. Friedman, *Martin Buber, The Life of Dialogue* (New York: Harper & Row, Publishers, 1960).

20. Heschel, *The Prophets*, p. 226.

21. New York: Farrar, Straus, & Giroux, Inc., 1966.

22. Heschel, *The Insecurity of Freedom* (New York: Farrar, Straus, and Giroux, Inc., 1966), pp. 14, 18.

23. Cf. his article "Situation Ethics" in *Norm and Context in Christian Ethics*, Paul Ramsey, Gene Outka, editors (New York: Charles Scribner's Sons, 1968), p. 331. Note: Among many other works by Fletcher, this article is chosen here because it seems to be a more balanced and mature statement than some of his earlier writings and manifests his concern to meet some of the criticism brought against him.

24. Cf. his *Ethics in a Christian Context* (New York: Harper & Row, Publishers, 1963), esp. Chap. 3 "What God is doing in the World", pp. 74–101.

25. Bernard Haring, *The Law of Christ*, Vol. I (Westminster, Md.: Newman Press, 1961), pp. 35–53, 63–73; cf. also Charles Curran, *Christian Morality Today*, (Notre Dame: Fides, 1966), Chapters 1–3.

26. Fletcher, *op. cit., loc. cit.*, p. 331.

27. *op. cit., loc. cit.*, pp. 348–49; cf. also G. F. Woods, *A Defense of Theological Ethics* (Cambridge, Mass.: Cambridge University Press, 1966).

28. *op. cit., loc. cit.*, p. 335.

29. *op. cit., loc. cit.*, p. 331.

30. *op. cit., loc. cit.*, p. 333, 348.

31. Fletcher, *op. cit., loc. cit.*, p. 333.

32. Cf. his book *The Secular City* (New York: The Macmillan Company, 1965).

33. Harvey Cox, "Tradition and the Future: II," in *Christianity and Crisis*, **27**: 17 (Oct. 16, 1967), pp. 227–31, esp. p. 227.

34. Cf. a book by that title, edited by James M. Gustafson and James T. Laney (New York: Harper & Row, Publishers, 1968), containing selections from major twentieth century theologians on the issue of being responsible in speech, love, and citizenship.

35. A frequently quoted phrase coming from the writings of Dietrich Bonhoeffer; Cf. especially his *Letters and Papers From Prison* (New York: The Macmillan Company, 1962).

36. M. Moinuddin Siddiqui, "Moral Teachings of Islam" in *Islamic Correspondence Course* (Fort Collins, Colo.: The Muslim Students Association).

37. Cf. Isma'il Rāgī al Fārūqī, "Islam" in *The Great Asian Religions* (New York: The Macmillan Company, 1969), pp. 307–18.

38. Cf. for example, Ernst Benz *Evolution and Christian Hope*, (New York: Doubleday & Company, Inc., 1968), esp. chap. VIII; Cf. also Frederick Elder, *Crisis in Eden*, (Nashville: Abingdon Press, 1970).

39. Cf. Jurgen Moltmann, *Theology of Hope* (New York: Harper and Row, Publishers, 1967), and E. Schillebeeckx, *God: The Future of Man* (New York: Sheed & Ward, 1968), esp. Chap. 6 on the new image of God.

40. Cf. "Port Huron Statement" in A. K. Bierman, and J. A. Gould, *Philosophy for a New Generation* (New York: The Macmillan Company, 1970), p. 36 ff. Cf. also Michael Novak, *A Theology for Radical Politics* (New York: Herder and Herder, Inc.: 1969), and Robert J. Lifton, "The Young and the Old" (Notes on a New History), in *The Atlantic Monthly*, **224**: 3 (Sept., 1969), pp. 47–54, and **224**: 4 (October, 1969), pp. 83–88.

chapter three

People

LET THE TERM "PEOPLE" stand for the meaning we assign to ourselves. That is, let it equal what we understand ourselves to be, or that which we intend to be. When speaking about man, we must remember that we already have a host of existing and well-established notions. Everyday language is sprinkled with references to human nature, being human, personal, and so on. The organized disciplines of knowledge have equally abundant sets of meanings, including everything from the classifications of zoology through those of psychology and sociology to the more poetic designations of the arts. The term "people" embraces this whole spectrum, without indicating a preference for one over the others.

However, such a term is not commonly used in either ordinary or scholarly discussions about the meaning of man. Consequently, it may have the favorable result of promoting a fresh look at what it means to be human, but only if we first clarify the precise way it is being used in this study.

The Meaning of the Factor Called "People"

When we ask that "people" be allowed to represent the meaning we assign to ourselves, we thereby allude to an understanding of ourselves acquired through either highly personal judgment or belief in the judgment of others. Self-understanding attained through the first route is generally the result of a serious effort to heed the admonition "know thyself." Yet, the understanding of ourselves is rarely, if ever, an unaided and exclusively individual procedure. It also implies the presence and influence of others, who assist us in both asking and answering the questions that lead to self-understanding.

Therefore, the "people" factor must be seen in a binocular manner, from the viewpoints of both personal assessment and that of others. In order to understand what we intend to summarily signify under the rubric "people" we must, therefore, clarify the kinds of judgment arising from this dual source.

Personal self-understanding. If and when someone understands himself in a relatively individual and unaided process of judgment, he might go through a process called "emerging self-consciousness." In general terms, this would consist in a series of stages, successively more integrated and unified than the initial polyform awareness with which we all begin. The purely experiential awareness which accompanies being alive is rather chaotic and disjointed, crying out for some organizing effort on our part. Perceptions, sensations, emotions and conations can be scattered and diffuse with no organizing symbol, or they can be grouped with the simple subject-symbol "I." "I" am the one who saw, felt, heard, wanted, was hurt, and so on. But differentiation is both possible and desirable, distinguishing kinds, qualities and levels of experiences. If we sort our sensations, we may begin to identify some experiences as biological, others as aesthetic, still others as rational, and so on. Once having distinguished our experiences and identified them, a reunification is demanded, and the possibilities of integrating signs like "my heart, my mind, my body" have appeal inasmuch as they effectively bring together a relatively homogeneous set of experiences under a single heading.

A model of rational self-consciousness. One model of the process involved in self-understanding is called the emergence of rational self consciousness.[1] According to this model, we emerge from the scattered awareness proper to experience through a more integrating rational grasp of our experience to a crowning awareness of self as subject and potential integrator of all prior levels of consciousness. This is a progression from the awareness of acting and being acted upon to insights giving unity and coherence to these experiences to a culminating judgment of self as conscious integrator of all that one experiences.

When growing up we learn to say "I feel, I understand, I want" with little if any integrated self consciousness. But, as self-awareness emerges, the presumption is that a conscious experiencing, understanding and choosing verify the symbols learned earlier.

If we are fully cognizant, we have to consider two additional factors, namely, the relational and the problematic aspects of our experiences. Our experiences are always in relationship to something or someone, and are always characterized by difficulties or problems, which, if potentially soluble, are not in fact either easily or always resolved.

The relational characteristic.   In the first place, all of our awareness is relational, but most especially so in the matter of assigning a meaning to our existence. It seems unlikely that anyone would claim to know what it is to be human apart from others with whom we identify, or from whom we learn to be skillful in both naming and using the capacities we have. In the second place, life with others presumes some institutionalized patterns of existence, and they in turn presuppose some organized sets of meanings, including of course the meaning of "people." This point will be treated more fully when we turn our attention to the second and social source of judgments about man. For the moment, relatedness is mentioned simply to balance the statements about self-awareness arising from one's own personal emergence to self-consciousness.

The problematic characteristic.   A second aspect of rational self-consciousness is that it is problematic, laced with difficulties and mistakes. No one seems able to completely avoid oversights of data, errors in identifying relationships, and jumping to conclusions. Utilizing the preceding model of the process of self-understanding, we can identify several areas where we might default in self-awareness. For example, when consciousness emerges from the experiences of living to insights and symbols that identify and integrate these experiences, we may err in various ways. It might be a case of insufficient experiential data, as in the case of a twelve-year-old who identifies his whole life's experiences without ever having fallen in love with a woman. Or, it might be a matter of an ill-chosen symbol to give coherence to one's experiences and insights, such as "Joey, the Mechanical Boy" who identified himself as a machine needing a constant source of electrical current.[2] A final and very plentiful source of difficulties is found in our efforts in verifying conclusions about ourselves and our meaning. This dimension of consciousness is simply riddled with opportunities for misunderstanding. Since verification requires the answering of all relevant questions, it takes time, effort and honesty. Yet, seldom, but by no means always, do we take such pains. Rationalization, renunciation of the effort required, and oversight of significant challenges throw shadows on an otherwise clear landscape.

However, the story of the problematic aspect of self-awareness is only partly told when we have seen the intellectual difficulties involved. There are others, often more radical and persistent, arising from the fact that we are both the playwrights and actors in the drama of our living. We do not simply experience and try to integrate and understand. We live, which implies writing our scripts, setting our scenarios, and playing our roles before an audience. Living and acting tend to get ahead of our thinking about it, precipitating action based on the best available judgments. Commitments are made and our audiences develop expectations, both of which make for tension between our knowing and our doing. As life moves along, it gets ever more difficult to revamp either our understanding or our styles of life, and nearly impossible to do both without dramatic breaks with past and present patterns of life.

Consequently, some kind of self-reform or conversion is required, sometimes more radical than at others, but a seemingly constant process for one who would emerge as rationally self-conscious, capable of integrating experience, thought and activity.

Self-understanding from others. When a baby is born he is cradled in the arms of people who have long held some particular meaning of being human. He is wrapped in symbols arising from the experience of others, and his behavior is patterned on concrete plans constructed from the thoughts of other human beings. It is generally beneficial for the child born in southwestern summer heat to have his experiences of heat and cold arranged for him by mechanical air-conditioning. It is also helpful to be met with elaborate and culturally imbedded arrangements that help us understand ourselves, but it is not without problems since it is based on the thoughts and experiences of others.

The child gets help in making sense out of his first experiences. Parents and elders provide names for things, judgments of truth and value, and organized routines of living at home, in school, and at church. In fact, this arranging of the child's life is so thorough and all-pervasive that his honest elders will someday have to warn him that "know thyself" includes as well an imperative to know how his self-knowledge has already been constructed by others. By the time critical self-consciousness comes to bloom, young people have already taken on the clothing of a civilization. They use the symbols others have found meaningful to identify their experiences. They think the thoughts which they have been taught are correct. They operate on the basis and within the limits of existing institutions, which arose from the plans and procedures of their predecessors.

However, as youth's critical powers sharpen, a decision looms on the horizon. Some will see it as a polar choice between an absolute affirmation of the truth and validity of what has been inherited, or an absolute rejection of it all, initiating a search for a truer and more valid position. As one's own experience and insights quicken, inherited symbols will inevitably seem inadequate. The experience of life in the electric age will necessarily provoke different symbols of being human, symbols that will sometimes clash with the presently accepted set, and this tension will produce gaps along the continuum of people old and young. If youth is met with inflexible attitudes and past symbols are surrounded with an aura of mystery, suspicion will be aroused. If they discover that traditional interpretations of man are held valid solely because of their vested interests in present socio-political structures, the tension will mount to the point of conflict and even revolution.

What is at stake in this process, if only unconsciously attended, is irresist-ability to change. Societies, and their institutionalized meanings, have every bit, if not more, the same need for reform and conversion that char-acterized the problem of individual consciousness. Societies are but aggre-gates of individuals sharing a relatively common experience, agreeing upon unifying symbols to give it coherence, and sanctioning a set of structures that make living less troublesome. Therefore, they too need a periodic overhaul of meanings, as well as changes in personnel and instruments. But they find it hard to get to it, difficult to assign its responsibility to any definite group, and, therefore, frequently neglect the task. Hence, the symptoms of trouble in social operation are, as in individuals, either ignored or ratio-nalized. Just as personal questions and warnings are ignored by individuals, so too are social prophets and gadflies smothered by people gathered in communities.

The preceding processes are identified in the sociology of knowledge[3] as those called 1. *externalization,* 2. *objectivation,* 3. *internalization,* and the correlative back-up procedures of 4. *legitimation,* and 5. *universe-maintenance.* The first three are ways of accounting for the fact that basically subjective meanings become acknowledged as objective realities. The question behind this account is "how do people come to their common-sense conclusions about life, man, and reality?" The hypothesis is that they have taken on (*internal-ized*) the existing set of recipes for living effectively. This seems inevitable, at least at this present stage of human psychic development. For man would otherwise be immobilized and unable to operate. Yet, when one accepts the beliefs, myths, maxims and values that constitute recipe knowledge, he thereby implicitly assents to some other person's judgment. And the intersubjective pressures from home, school, church and society are such that they promote this kind of assent. To give it is to belong, but the with-holding of it is tantamount to social self ostracization.

One of the problems associated with socially sanctioned common sense is that its original meanings get submerged or forgotten in the course of time. What were once very meaningful verbal symbols *externalized* by sen-sitive and talented interpreters become diluted or lost in the process of insti-tutionalization. It would be safe to say that Socrates and Jefferson would be shocked to see what social *objectivation* has done with their subjective understandings of man, freedom, and government. As symbolic meanings are given objective rational content, and built up into plans and procedures, they tend to diverge more and more from the interpretations of their origi-nators. People who read the Dialogues of Plato and the Papers of Jefferson will find any number of contradictions between them and the social struc-tures which are supposed to be faithful reproductions of their convictions.

Consequently, since upcoming generations will not be familiar with the biography of its society's recipe knowledge, and idiosyncratic individuals will take issue with the adequacy of such knowledge, society will require various forms of *legitimation* and *universe-maintenance*. Officialdom will designate orthodox legitimators, who will be vested with the right and duty to proclaim the true story, to demonstrate its validity, and give credibility to its continuing role as the legitimate meaning of what we experience. Dissenters will be given therapy in various forms of pacific or punitive re-socialization, and contrary interpretations will be ruled out as heretical and unorthodox. Since common sense, and its recipe knowledge, is by its very nature pre-reflective and pre-theoretical, thoughtful men will always need either therapy or liquidation. And this may be the reason why western society has "fed the hemlock" to many more than the famous Athenian who found he could not live an unexamined life.

When societies are highly organized, as have been most western societies, they not only tend to resist change, but also develop machinery to maintain and legitimate the universe of meaning on which they are based. Consequently some rightly point to the fact that the meaning assigned to man is something of a "self-fulfilling prophecy"[4] which brings about not only a state of affairs but also a state of consciousness (through introjected meaning), both of which give witness to the common notions of what it means to be human. Optimistic views of man give rise to trusting institutions and optimism in the consciousness of those in the society, but the reverse is true in societies built upon dim views of man.

Since the knowledge underpinning societies in their fund of common sense is largely preconceptual and habitual, science finds itself often at odds with community judgments about man and his values. As one contemporary biologist puts it,

> The very temper and attitude of mind that permit science to flourish must in themselves produce conflicts with many traditional values. . . . Inevitably it is disturbing, for it clashes with traditional ways of thought and dogmatic belief, which are deeply rooted; these are the product of generations of men, and they are charged with powerful emotions. These traditional attitudes are generally the product of instinctive wisdom; they have grown up without logical foundation, as useful beliefs generally do, but with profound relevance to human needs in the society in which they arose. As the world changes, these beliefs may become irrelevant, sometimes dangerously irrelevant; and in our time such changes are brought about predominantly by the progress of science and technology.*

Much more needs to be understood about these processes of socially held "truths," but this is, unfortunately, a poor place to do it. Our questions, and the answers we seek in this chapter are primarily concerned with the

---

* J. T. Edsall, "Biology and Human Values," in *Knowledge and the Future of Man*, Walter J. J. Ong, ed., (New York: Holt, Rinehart and Winston, Inc., 1968), p. 161.

interactions between factors in this social body of knowledge. We are trying to establish a meaning of the "people" factor, by discussing the two general sources (personal, social) of our understanding of what we are as human beings. The sociology of knowledge aids us in understanding the social source, and provides detail as to how we acquire our common-sense knowledge of peoplehood. We leave further investigation of this point to other studies in order to apply what we already know to the question at hand, and now proceed to examine the ways in which religion influences the two sources of self-understanding, working toward the point where the religiously interpreted factor of "people" can be seen in systematic interdependence with process and principles in religious ethics.

Religion's Shaping of Our Self-understanding

By now it should be clear that this writer is convinced of the fact that artistic symbols are by far the most influential fashioners of our self-understanding. The songs sung to us, pictures shown us, and the literature written for us provide an ample supply of images of man.[5] Literature, above all, seems to be the homeland for images of man, at least from the sixteenth century to the beginnings of this century in the West.

Granting these assumptions, it is but a short step to understanding how religious insight helps fashion some of these images. Maurice Friedman surveys the present field of offering in contemporary western images of man, and identifies several of the alternatives as decidedly religious in origin. There can be no doubt that The Modern Prometheus, The Modern Job, The Modern Mystic, The Modern Saint, The Modern Gnostic, and The Theological Existentialist arise from Greek, Jewish and Christian religious traditions.[6] Furthermore, the Eastern religions may be said to have even tighter connections to the art and literature that molds man's self-understanding in those cultures. This can be seen in the evidence supporting the truism that, in the East, religion and culture are inseparably intertwined, while the dichotomy of sacred and profane has been both the child and burden of western thought.

So far we have merely noted the fact that religion provides much of the imagery that *individuals* find in art and literature. But the rest of the story is also important, namely, the way in which religious "fictions" permeate the body of recipe knowledge in the community of common sense, and thereby exert a profound influence on the way we understand ourselves. As preconscious and prereflective, common sense consists of a treasury of "judgments" about the solutions to everyday problems. It is a type of knowledge which is preserved and communicated through beliefs and values, maxims and slogans, people and institutionalized procedures. It is highly useful knowledge, solving problems rapidly, forestalling further questions that would challenge its validity, and providing a stable platform of the "obvious" from which we may operate with ample insulation from the pain of doubt, uncertainty and the absurd.

Religion plays a dual role in relation to this body of knowledge, acting as a cooperator in its creation and occasionally attempting to either reform or destroy it. Religious insight and teaching help build the fabric of meaning in a society, but, in their more prophetic moments, likewise attempt to subvert and modify it.

(1) The *construction* of what common sense recognizes as the meaning of man is assisted by religious *mythos* in several ways. One vehicle for influencing our self-understanding has been the idealizing of certain prominent human beings or culture heroes. All the founders of world religions have become ideal types, and many leaders in each of these religions have become culture heroes, each according to the value preferences of the culture in question. These models, endorsed by some religion, have often become the paradigm profiles of what it is to be human, reinforced with glowing, if sometimes inaccurate, accounts of their amazing lives. Another way in which religious *mythos* helps construct social reality and its knowledge is by way of being incarnated in social plans and procedures. Examples abound, such as the Muslim practice of polygamy and the Hindu caste system. Judaism and Christianity are given credit for "ethicizing" western civilization, shaping its values and beliefs, helping man understand himself and his responsibilities. Western courts of law, business practices, marriage laws and others, are all examples of social procedures ethicized by Jewish and Christian values. These procedures, in turn, are often responsible for helping shape our awareness of who we are in relation to others. Finally, religious *mythos* helps construct common-sense meanings of man by providing the public with an array of maxims which embody a view of man. Recipes for the so-called tight spots in life are always in demand. Religion often meets this common need with axiomatic wisdom from both oral and written sources. Axioms from the Wisdom books of the Bible is one such popular source, while others are maxims from religiously-oriented ethnic groups. Some of these maxims might include:

> "The poor man's wisdom keeps his head erect, and gives him a place with the great."[7]
> Better to have a worn but clean pair of pants than an expensive but soiled pair.
> It's better to die with a good reputation than with millions in the bank.
> Better to live and fight another day.

Each one of these axioms implies a view of man, some unstated but necessary understanding about what we are or should be. And this implied judgment is both the warrant for the axiom and the image of man that is communicated by the slogan. Even when inspected closely the implied notions of man are barely discernible. Yet, this is precisely why they are so effectively communicated among those who prefer to live almost exclusively on the level of preconscious common sense. If they were highly visible they would also be very debatable. Debate takes time, and critical reflection slows us down; so action-minded people will generally prefer the slogan to the nuanced notion. Since they do, a variety of meaning-makers, including the religious, can shape their understanding of themselves through a variety of action axioms which embody implied judgments about man.

(2) However, in addition to helping create social understanding of man, religion also aids in *destroying and recreating* accepted meanings. In this pro- phetic role, religious interpreters, behaving like gadflies, call the men of common sense to critical re-evaluation. They point up the contradictions between social practices and the community's beliefs. They demonstrate the ways in which life has degenerated, falling short of the dignity of man, draining quality from his day-to-day dealings with other men. They recall the past, "more glorious" days, or call for a recreated future, a better day to come.

In so doing religious prophets call men out of the quagmire of precon- scious and unreflective judgment. They invite critical reflection on the dis- torted meanings that have led to our present problems, and suggest the adoption of either more traditional or entirely novel meanings leading to a solution.

In these ways, religion plays an important, and in some cultures, a fairly exclusive role in the shaping of our self-understanding of what it means to be human.

The Function of the "People" Factor in Religious Ethics

Thus far we have considered both a meaning of "people" and the ways in which religion influences its meaning. We should now try to determine how the meaning given to people acts as a factor in religious ethics. This will be done in a manner comparable to the way process was considered in the prior chapter. The meaning assigned to people will be viewed in its inter-relationship to the meanings of process and principles in two sets of examples, from both Eastern and Western traditions in religious ethics.

THE PEOPLE FACTOR IN SOME
EASTERN FORMS OF RELIGIOUS ETHICS

For the sake of clarity and ease of understanding, the examples used in this chapter will be the same as those of the preceding and following chapters. In this way, the reader will be able to compare the comments made about process and principles with those made here about the people factor in these traditions.

Confucianism. When Confucius set out to correct the practices of a disturbingly corrupt Chinese society in the sixth century B.C., he placed such emphasis on man and his perfectibility that it carried through the Confucian tradition as one of its key factors. Unlike some of his successors, who will be mentioned shortly, Confucius dis not spend much time debating the question about man's basic goodness or wickedness.

The *Analects*, probably polished by his disciples' disciples, reveal Confucius' basic concern about man in his work. In the *Analects* X:12 we find this statement: "When the stables were burned down, on returning from court, Confucius asked: 'Was anyone hurt?' He did not ask about the horses."[8] This humanitarian concern was coupled with a basic optimism in Confucius' thinking. He believed that men were very much alike by nature and that learning and practice were what distinguished them.

The man who blended the art of living harmoniously with his basic nature was styled the "gentleman," who is both scholarly and political, knowing the principles of right living and taking responsibility seriously both at home and in society at large. In the view of Confucius, this gentleman was one who reached human fulfillment by acting in accordance with the will of Heaven (the *Tao* characterized as a personal, guiding Providence). The gentleman could discover Heaven's will in tradition, custom, and the collective experience of men, all of which confirm the *Tao* or moral law contained in man's heart.

With the impetus provided by Confucius, this ideal of peoplehood was given lasting symbolic form in the description of the "gentleman." However, the meaning of man or human nature became an issue for Confucian leaders in the centuries following the teachings of Master K'ung. In the fourth to third centuries B.C., Meng Tzu or Mencius taught that man was born with the beginnings of virtue and an inclination to goodness. He predicated a state of original goodness animated by a childlike heart at birth, and believed that evil resulted by neglecting or abusing this basic innate good nature of ours.

This most optimistic view of man was quickly challenged by the third century Confucian Hsün Tzu, whose experiences with crumbling feudal states convinced him that something more than a mere return to older golden ages (either social or personal) was illusory. With blunt realism he took a stand opposing Mencius' teaching on man's nature, and argued that goodness was not an original endowment lost through abuse or neglect, but rather a hard-won habit gained through demanding conscious activity. Man, he thought, was like a warped piece of wood, which could be straightened through the instruction of teachers offering principles in conformity to the Way (*Tao*).[9]

In the work of Hsün Tzu, as in that of Mencius, we find the traditional Confucian ideal of "the gentleman." Even after debates about the original goodness of man, the understanding of what man could and should become was still cast in the traditional terminology. Hsün Tzu found fault with Mencius' teaching because it portrayed man as one who is basically good, and, therefore, capable of learning. As Hsün Tzu saw it, Mencius had failed to distinguish between human nature and conscious activity. The natural inclinations of man appeared to Hsün Tzu as primarily emotional, the most obvious part of human nature's inclinations. He saw them as naturally inclining man to behavior without courtesy or humility, both of which are quite foreign to the emotional drives of man. In contrast with Mencius, he did not agree that the principles of good behavior arose from human nature, even when there is no neglect or abuse of the basic goodness Mencius had identified. Principles come from conscious activity according to Hsün Tzu, for conscious discrimination is the hallmark of man, setting him off from the beasts, leading to the teaching and learning of principles in conformity with the *Tao*.[10]

While retaining the customary Confucian ideal of the gentleman, Hsün Tzu idealized neither the past societies nor the childhood of man, and consequently arrived at principles similar to those of Confucius and Mencius, with a very different understanding of human nature. The functional inter-relationship of his people factor with his reinterpretation of the Confucius-Mencius process factor is very important, and helps illuminate the nuanced differences of opinion between the three great minds of early Confucian ethical teaching.

In the centuries following these early thinkers, the optimism of Mencius seemed to prevail as the dominant interpretation of man. The people factor in Confucian thinkers during the Sung dynasty (10th to 13th centuries A.D.) demonstrates the traditional concern for culture, with man at the center of their teachings. Chu Hsi of the Neo-Confucian School of Reason elaborates on Mencius' declaration of the goodness of human nature.[11] Wang Yang-ming (Ming dynasty of the 14th to 17th centuries) acts as spokesman for the School of Intuition and develops the traditional notion of a universal moral law immanent in man, setting human nature up as basically good and inclined in the right direction, but capable of being derailed by conscious activity which often distorts one's innate sense of right and wrong.[12]

If we were to give a summary generalization of the traditional interpretation Confucians give to the meaning of man, it would have to focus on the ideal to be achieved rather than on the nature of man, about which there have been some major disagreements. With regard to the ideal, however, all Confucians seem to have held up the goal of becoming a gentleman, or a superior man. Echoing many of the aristocratic sensitivities of Confucius and his followers, the ideal man is the self-contained and perfectly harmonious man, one who, like the *Tao* itself, achieves a perfect harmony between one's inner and outer lives. The gentleman, then, is one whose motives would be consistent with his manners, a man of integrity whose words and actions are accurate indicators of what is in his mind and heart.[13]

Taoism. The people factor in the Taoist tradition is often contrasted with the sober responsible scholar-citizen of Confucianism. Some like to emphasize the Taoist ideal as that of a wise man, preferring solitude to social involvement, one who seeks release from the cares of responsibility, and yearns for solitary moments of intoxication with nature.

Generalizations like this hold up in part because they accurately reflect the whimsical and fanciful character of Taoism as contrasted with the relatively somber emphases of the Confucian tradition. In lines of delightful poetry and allegory, Taoist wise men have promoted ideals of cooperation with nature (*Tao*) and have satirized the efforts of those who wasted their energies in tiresome activity interfering with nature. Chuang Tzu, for example, thought the work of the debater Hui Shih pointless and described him as a man trying to silence an echo by shouting at it.[14]

Specific examples of Taoist teaching about the meaning of man bear out the truth of the generalization just mentioned. In the *Tao-te-ching*, attributed to Lao-tzu, we find a human ideal of primitive simplicity, which emphasizes the need to perfect one's own purity and intelligence, and nowhere puts human fulfillment in terms of learning moral and social principles. The fourth century (B.C.) Chuang-tzu carries this tradition to a more elaborate and explicit statement, extolling the ideal of the free individual. As contrasted with the earlier Taoist interpretation setting forth the ideal of unsophisticated simplicity, Chuang-tzu takes a more skeptical attitude toward man considering him unnatural and artificial. In his opinion, we cannot simply return to or take on an attitude of primitive simplicity, but rather must work at liberating ourselves from the confusions which make up our convictions and values.

The ideal for human life is the way of the sage, the "true man", the one who is liberated from his partial views of truth and falsity and his cloudy values of justice and injustice. This true man or sage understands and lives in the underlying unity of life, the *Tao*, and thereby finds tranquility. He has achieved a mystical union with the Way (*Tao*), undergoes no change, and thus has gained a kind of immortality which transcends both life and death. He no longer wears himself out in searching, investigating and striving; he simply lets things be, resting in the realization that all is one and that non-interference with nature is, in the long run, the most effective kind of behavior.

Hinduism-Buddhism. The people factor in the religious tradition called Hinduism and its "protesting" Buddhist progeny is both fascinating and complex. The meaning assigned to man in these streams of religious interpretation has a history which is both very ancient and rich in diversity. In terms of the last chapter's outline of the threefold path to salvation we can schematize the people factor in Hindusim-Buddhism as follows:

1. In *Karma Marga* man is seen principally as the man of action and duty.
2. In *Jnana Marga* the emphasis is on the knowing man.
3. In *Bhakti Marga* it is the loving and compassionate man who is extolled.

As a schema, however, the above is open to misinterpretation unless we note that one emphasis does not necessarily exclude all the others. In fact, the history of Hinduism reveals that emphasis on insight and knowledge did not completely eradicate the importance of action and duty, but added a new dimension to it and placed the primary emphasis on the knowing man without excluding the ideal of *Karma.* The same can be said about the ideal of *bhakti marga* which summarizes without ignoring the importance of both action and insight, but puts a special emphasis on the desirability of becoming a compassionate man.

Jainism and Buddhism arose in the India of the sixth century B.C., the time in which we identify the beginnings of the emphasis on the way of knowledge (*jnana marga*). It seems that leaders in these two Hindu-based sects were most seriously opposed to the common man's understanding of Brahmanic teaching about obligatory actions and duties. The ritualism of the prior period had exaggerated the importance of ceremonial killing and sacrifice, ritual priesthood and numerous acts of household ritual. Quite naturally, the ordinary Hindu understood himself in terms of what he was to become as depicted in the ideal of the man of action and duty in the ceremonial sense. Reacting to this, both the Buddha and the Mahavira laid more emphasis on knowledge and self discipline as the ideal of the true Aryan way. Their teachings focused on the experience of suffering, its causes, and held out the ideal of a liberation made possible through insight.

Subsequent developments in Hinduism (especially in the *Upanishads*) helped support a similar emphasis in the parent religious body, such that both Hinduism and Buddhism clung to a people ideal called the *arhat.* The *arhat,* sometimes called saint, is one who, through his own efforts, becomes a holy man and is no longer subject to the cycle of life and death. He can achieve *nirvana* or salvation even while living, but does so only through the highest degree of self-controlled practice in the physical and mental skills leading to enlightenment.

Changes of emphasis occurred again in the first few centuries A.D. and a people ideal of a helping man began to take hold. The primary meaning of man shifted during the period emphasizing devotion and compassion (*bhakti marga*). The ideal of escape or liberation from the round of rebirths through personal enlightenment no longer held the primacy of attention as a people ideal. In addition to it, there appeared an ideal extolling the man who postponed his liberation for the sake of others. Such a man was called a *bodhisattva* (Buddha-to-be) and characterized as a mediator or helper to others seeking *nirvana*. It is really quite significant that this ideal occurred in connection with the Mahayana Buddhist ideal of universal salvation, moving away from the earlier more individualistic ideal of salvation through *personal* achievement.

If you expand this sketch of three different people factors, all of which are not mutually exclusive but put emphasis on different characteristics, you can begin to understand the fascinating but complex differences of opinion in Hinduism and Buddhism. If you also link the changes in the people factor with corresponding changes in the process factor you can find many examples of the functional inter-relationships between the two in Hindu and Buddhist teachings about human behavior.

THE PEOPLE FACTOR IN SOME
WESTERN FORMS OF RELIGIOUS ETHICS

Jewish ethics since Kant.   The predominant emphasis in traditional Jewish interpretations of man has been one which emphasized the unity or wholeness of man. By unity they have not understood uniformity, such that man was considered to be uniformly of one quality such as material or spiritual, but rather that man cannot be divided abstractly into body-spirit components. Hence, the common Jewish interpretations of the meaning of man usually insist that people be considered as concrete unities, which, if not always fully harmonious, at least should strive toward this ideal.

Traditional Judaism clearly recognizes that man is troubled with tensions which pull him in opposing directions, giving him some difficulty in achieving the harmony and unity he desires. Most Jewish thinkers describe this as a state of being torn between two *yetzers*, one's good and evil impulses. They see man, for example, caught between the pull of material and immaterial forces, strained by opposing desires for personal independence and the demands made on him in social living.

The remarkable thing about the Jewish tradition, however, is that it has usually been able to view these tensions dialectically without falling into the either-or pitfalls of some forms of western thought. It has never seen man one-sidedly as either "good *yetzer*" or "bad *yetzer*," totally material or fully spiritual, either completely autonomous or entirely subservient, but has retained a way of thinking about man in concrete terms describing a unity in the midst of diverse experiences.

Moreover, the traditional teaching of the Jewish faith has held up both the possibility and ideal of harmonizing the tensions we experience. If Jews expected such harmony only in the end of days, its partial realizations were the task of every day. The search for learning and the practice of justice carried on before God are the classical recommendations of a faith in man's ability to transcend the various tensions in life. By sublimating the evil impulse, man can rise above the downward pull of life and transcend some of its limitations, if, of course, life is consciously directed toward God.[15]

The rabbinic hero-image, one of the classical Jewish models of what man can become, is a blending of the images of prophet, priest and sage from biblical literature. The rabbinic hero takes the priestly regulations of purity and charity upon himself, as well as the prophetic role of confronting the social realities of his day, not to mention the sage's equally demanding tasks of prayer and study leading to wisdom.

Functionally related to this interpretation of what man may become, there is a set of Jewish principles which guide men toward the ideal of harmonized human existence. In both Torah and Talmud, the Jew who would be faithful is advised to follow the way of the Law. The Law exacts a discipline of prayer and learning, the practice of purity and charity, the pursuit of peace and justice in the community, as well as in the raising of one's family. It endorses the unifying of the rational and the emotional with the mystical attitude of living in covenant with God, hence furthering the ideal of harmonizing all of man's capabilities.

1. *Hermann Cohen and Leo Baeck*, following the Kantian emphasis on the primacy of ethics, defined the "essence of Judaism" as ethical monotheism, and gave much more attention to law (principles) than to interpretations of man. That is not to say, however, that they do not have a view of man that functionally coheres with their understanding of law's central role. In fact, both Baeck and Cohen base their interpretation of Judaism on the Kantian view of man as a being who has a "sense of the ethical." Baeck goes beyond Cohen to add a dimension of man which he calls religious consciousness. In both, however, a view of man is a necessary factor in support of their notions on the origin and function of ethical principles. If there is no source but man, they reason, he must be capable of developing these principles; he must have the moral "sense" that yields these ethical norms. Therefore, we should conclude that the ethical systems of Cohen and Baeck, while focused primarily on principles, are nevertheless dependent upon a presupposed notion of people.[16]

2. *Mordecai Kaplan*, founder of Jewish Reconstructionism, has a much more explicit view of people, and one which plays a commanding role in his ethical system. In fact, the "people" factor seems to be the central point from which radiate all the other elements in his ethical thought.

His focus is on man and what contributes to his welfare. From that basic principle he argues to the fact that community fulfills man, his needs and hopes, but that all communities (including governments) are under man's control. A community, or people, needs a land and a law, but both must serve the people. For Kaplan, a people is necessarily prior to its religion, which supplements the essentially human creation of community. Law is folk-created and by no means a form of heavenly compulsion. Since man and his welfare are primary, all legal and political instruments of this well-being are to be tested by the central criterion identified here as his people factor.[17]

3. *Martin Buber* likewise places the people factor in the forefront of his ethics, but in a very different way. When he wrote his philosophical masterwork *I and Thou* in 1923, he did so out of a context of drastic change in Europe. The older value systems had come crashing down, and men were engaged in a somewhat frenzied search for new ones. Buber hoped to preserve man's nobility and prevent him from being reduced to just one more scientific object of research. Consequently, he wrote with passion, demonstrating the difference between the treatment of man as a "Thou" and that which reduced him to an "It." He viewed the latter interpretation of man as the cause of the hollowness and emptiness so plaintively decried in the poetry of T.S. Eliot, and trusted the former view to provide a gurantee for rescuing man's self-estimate from the scalpel of scientism. He reasoned that, if people met as persons in I-Thou encounters, they could count on mutual respect and reverence, the qualities which alone give birth to humane forms of social existence.

Principles are man-created protections for the nobility we possess as persons, but are fashioned "in dialogue with God," the ground of all I-Thou encounters. As noted in the preceding chapter, the covenant tie with God is the normative relationship. This relational event, symbolized in Sinai, is ever present, and through it, men find the ability to deal with each other as persons rather than things. From both the divine and human relationships we can, says Buber, find principles which bind us to each other in communities of peace and justice.[18]

4. The neo-orthodox Jewish theologian *Abraham J. Heschel* gives little place to such highly rational notions of man as expressed by Cohen, Baeck and Kaplan. What is understood and to be said about man is, for Heschel, more a result of certain partial truths realized in moments of intense clarity, than it is a consequence of a human insight into and structuring of the notion of human nature.

Accordingly, Heschel likes to refer to the "sacred image of man," a partial grasp of what man is, realized in the proclamation of *Genesis* 1:26 ff. Man, made in the image and likeness of God, as proclaimed in *Genesis* is *haggadah* (the proclamation of good news). As Heschel himself admits, this statement conceals more than it reveals. No man knows God as He is, except to say He is divine and we are human, and that does not tell us very much about ourselves or how we are "like" God.

What is revealed here, he says, is a common concern, or a task commonly assumed by God and man in relationship. Unlike that part of the Western

Christian tradition which identifies one particular characteristic of man as the "likeness," Heschel includes in it both body and soul, the sage as well as the fool, saint and sinner alike. The likeness, he claims, is not *in* man; it *is* man, in both his grandeur and his insignificance.

In another series of biblical texts on man's sonship (e.g. *Malachi* 2:10, and *Job* 31:15) he finds further partial insights about man. Man is what he is because God is at stake in what we experience, and our ultimate confrontation is not with the world but with God. Therefore, sonship implies more than mere dependence. It means that man is confronted by God as responsible for nothing less than God Himself![19]

Combining these two characteristics of man into a coherent scheme, man is seen as having both a dignity and a responsibility that accords with the image of him in biblical proclamation (*haggadah*). It is but a short step from this notion of people to principles functionally related to it such as the guideline contained in the following statement: "Man is called upon to act in the likeness of God. 'As He is merciful be Thou merciful' "[20]

For Heschel, then, *process* (God involved in human history), *people* (man confronted by God's presence as he acts), and *principles* (acting in the "likeness of God") are functionally related parts of a single mosaic, manifesting the presence of the religiously ethical in human life.

5. Before concluding our considerations of post-Kantian Jewish thought about man, we should mention, however briefly, the views of *Rabbi Joseph Baer Soloveitchik*. The other Jewish theologians just mentioned have based their understanding of man on the *haggadah*, but Soloveitchik has been building his theology on what is implied in Jewish *halakha* (instruction). Consequently, his interpretation of what it is to be human is quite different from those mentioned. While he is most like Heschel in his neo-orthodox stand on theological issues, his emphasis on the legal and socio-political materials of Jewish *halakha* is uniquely different.

Soloveitchik's view of man leans heavily on the phenomenon of loneliness. In this he is admittedly influenced by the thought of Ibsen and Kierkegaard, Scheler and Heidegger, finding the existential and phenomenological descriptions of man both accurate and helpful in describing man's predicament. His analysis of man builds on a series of "types" starting with the two Adams in the creation stories, he interprets man as maker-controller-user (Adam I), and yet submissive-accepting (Adam II). The characteristic typified in Adam I is man's outgoing and manipulative aspect, according to which he sets norms for himself, builds community, and strives to reach God. But Adam II typifies the other side of man, in which he accepts the world as it is, submits to God's call in the covenant and overcomes his loneliness in a genuine community of faith and friendship. *Halakhic* man overcomes this tension between his two sides by confronting life and channelling subjective faith into social and political structures. He does not retreat into the peace found in passive submission, but tries to transform his subjective and personal faith into specific institutions for life together with others.

For Soloveitchik, then, action in life is the result of principles and norms derived from two aspects of man. The specifically Jewish contribution comes as a result of the man of *halakha*, who builds his structures with faith, typified in the submissive-accepting Adam II. On this basis Soloveitchik not only provides an interpretation of "people," but also offers a criterion for evaluating principles. He would, for example, declare that norms and institutions which encourage man's world-building aspect are less valuable than those which emanate from his intersubjective side, thereby suggesting a way of discriminating between different principles as born of different aspects of man.[21]

Christian ethics since the reformation. When dealing with the Jewish interpretation of man it was both convenient and accurate to refer to a "normative strain" in Judaism which emphasizes the unity of man. In handling the materials from Christianity, however, references to any such norm would prove to be both distorted and unwieldy. Hence, we will refrain from any attempt at generalizing a "Christian view of man," except to note the usual reading of such a view by those who observe Christianity from the outside.

What they usually find evidenced on the surfaces of Christian faith is what we might term the "dualistic" interpretation of man. Observers of Christianity call attention to interpretations of human nature which emphasize the hellenistic view of a body-spirit split in man. They attribute this to a preoccupation with the doctrine of the Fall of Man (original sin) and the assumption of Greek categories of a neoplatonic variety into Christian doctrine. Paul and Augustine are generally credited with the principal responsibility for these emphases, mitigated in Catholicism by the Aristotelianism of Aquinas, but reemphasized for Protestantism by Luther, Calvin, and others in the tradition of the Reformation. The conclusion drawn by even the more than casual student of Christianity is that Christians consider man to be basically evil, and they find this conviction stated in crassly literal terms as well as in subtle inferences to the same effect.[22]

However, anyone who pursues the Christian interpretation of man more extensively will find two things to be true. First of all, since the Reformation at least, the differences in Christian views of man are more than simply subtle differences of the same pessimistic outlook. Secondly, changes in principles or guidelines for action have provoked many reworkings of the "official" view of man.

In order to follow some of the nuanced meanings of the Christian interpretation of man we will employ the four-fold schema used in the preceding chapter. While suffering the limitations proper to all schemata, this division will open up as many of the diverse Christian points of view as is possible within the scope of this study. In this way, then, we can at least get some basic understanding of the functional relationship of the people factor to the process factor in some systems of Christian ethics.

Those who prefer the symbols of creation-fall-redemption. It is important to remind ourselves at this point that the various Christian systems of ethics have a strong common bond giving Christ a central place in all ethical considerations. While they may have diverse understandings of his meaning and role in moral matters, Christian thinkers always attribute some kind of moral effectiveness to Christ.*

The diversity of interpretations can be considered in any number of ways, among which is the method utilized here. We are examining various schools of Christian ethics in terms of the symbols which they more commonly use in speaking about the difference Christ makes in morality. In these terms we are identifying a group of religious interpreters who seem to prefer the symbols of creation-fall-redemption, and who build on the belief that man stands related to God as Creator and Redeemer, with Christ acting as mediator of the Father in both these activities.

Arising from this preference is an interpretation of man, which forms the people factor in various ethical considerations of this school of thought. Taking the biblical stories of creation, fall, and redemption as a starting-point, one can develop a view of man seen as originally good, endowed with freedom and dignity. The symbol of the fall (variously interpreted as caused by forms of egoism and pride) yields another characteristic of man, which depicts him as guilty, wounded, estranged, or alienated from God. These two symbols (created and fallen) are but a preface to the specifically Christ-centered task of redeeming man. Variously interpreting the forgiving and reconciling activity of Christ, theologians in this school talk about man as one who has need of and access to the healing remedies for his fallen condition.

To this extent the position described above is commonly held by all four general strains of Christian ethics. What is unique and specific to the creation-fall-redemption school is its emphasis on man *in relation* to God, standing under divine judgment or "over against" God. They develop this basic premise to demonstrate that man becomes acquainted with himself, or his condition, through the saving work of Christ. Christ is depicted in the Pauline terms of "new man" or "second Adam" in whom man's relationship with the Father is both manifested and transformed. Theologians in this school then go on to show how man's estranged relationship with God is overcome by Christ and by our relationship to him.

The principal emphasis in this view of man is that he is dependent. Interpretations of man coming from science or philosophy and declaring

* Cf. Appendix A.

man to be autonomous are severely criticized by this school of thought. They reason that the only truly reliable information about man is that which is contained in this Christian revelation, without which man must necessarily misunderstand himself and all the judgments he fashions for his life.

There are some in this school who give outsiders reason to believe that Christians have a jaundiced view of man emphasizing his sinfulness and estrangement, but the notable thinkers in this school usually offer more balanced statements about man, and see him depending upon God for existence, forgiveness and rebirth. Such is the position of Karl Barth, one of the most respectable representatives of this emphasis. In what Barth has written we can find both highly nuanced statements of man's relationship of dependence,[23] and samples of the kinds of principles considered suitable to living up to this condition. For example, in a rather typical Barthian statement we find the following: "For the man who obediently hears the command of God is not in any position to consider why he must obey it."*

In terms of a systems approach to religious ethics, we can identify a functional connection between the factors in a school of Christian ethics which emphasizes the creation-fall-redemption symbols. This can be studied in the works of Karl Barth, as in others, and expressed in the following manner: the *process* in which man finds himself is one that is fashioned by the creating, sustaining and redeeming work of God; *people* are created, fallen, and redeemed, standing in a relationship of dependence on God, who both makes them and rescues them; the *principles* by which man directs his conscience and activity are norms endorsing obedience as the principal virtue of the dependent man.

Those emphasizing the symbol of justification. These people do not deny the beliefs implied in the symbols of creation-fall redemption, but simply attribute to the symbol of justification the power to tie together all other symbols into a coherent theological system. They prefer this particular biblical emphasis as their over-arching symbol and work out a coherent doctrine and ethic on its basis. By placing such emphasis on the symbol of justification, the religious ethicians in this school thereby commit themselves to statements about man which are consistent with the emphasis on the process of imputing justice to man.

Their people factor has a strong emphasis on the human situation of being declared or judged guilty before God. Man is in a sinful condition, but can be made just by a God who declares him to be forgiven and saved by faith in Jesus Christ. Promoters of this emphasis in Christian ethics do not, therefore, give much place to philosophies or psychologies of man. They do not seem interested in discussing man's moral development, or transformation in the mind and heart of man.

* Karl Barth, *Church Dogmatics* II/2, G. W. Bromiley and T. F. Torrance, eds., (Edinburgh: T. & T. Clark, Edinburgh, 1967), p. 522.

It is generally recognized that Martin Luther and most Lutheran theologians made some rather extravagant statements about man's depravity. We can find references to man as leprous and unclean in the writings of Luther himself as well as in the Formulary of Concord and the Augsburg Confession. Religious ethicians in this tradition are primarily concerned with the classical Reformation question "How can I be saved?" and respond by saying that we are saved through a trusting faith in the word proclaiming us to be free. This declaration is like the action of a judge rendering a sentence of "no longer guilty," but is extrinsic to man, not really changing his nature interiorly. Hence, these ethicians formulate ethical principles which remind man of his need to confess his sins, to walk in faith, and to be alert to the necessity of being constantly converted lest he fall back into sin. Human systems of ethics are considered illusory, leading man to think he can become just by his own efforts, and thus many justificationists insist that the Christian recognize that "true justification" comes only from God's declaration and one's faith in it, with all human ethics being considered inherently self-justifying and necessarily under divine judgment.

There is one very notable exception to this general run of justificationist thinking in the person of the twentieth-century American theologian, Reinhold Niebuhr. He seems to have preferred the justification symbolism on the whole, and was most anxious to put the spotlight on the problematical aspect of man's existence, but returned beyond Luther to Augustine as his principal inspiration for a doctrine of man. He was convinced that Luther had added nothing new to Augustine, and had, in fact, exaggerated the marred condition of man.[24] Niebuhr's aims were many, among which was an effort to explore the degree of fruitful interrelationship between Renaissance and Reformation insights about human nature.[25]

In Niebuhr's scheme the Christian view of man relates three aspects of human existence to each other. First of all, the symbol of the "image of God" stresses a lofty self-transcendence for man. Secondly, there is an insistence on man's finite and dependent nature. Thirdly, the cause of man's problems is identified as an "inevitable though not necessary" unwillingness to live as finite and dependent.[26] As he developed this schema, Niebuhr was careful to emphasize the biblical view of man as a creature in a basically good creation,[27] but then turns his attention to Man as Sinner, Original Sin and Man's Responsibility.[28]

Quantitatively speaking he spends much more time and space on man's problem (nearly two hundred pages on the sinful side, as opposed to ten or so pages on the created goodness aspect). This is understandable in view of the exaggerated optimism about man in his day, a naiveté which he wanted to chastise. We should also recall that the social and political problems of the thirties in America gave him an abundance of empirical evidence of man's difficulties, and inclined him to utilize the perspective suggested by the biblical symbols of sin and justification. His analysis of man is, therefore, built primarily, but not exclusively, on the doctrine of original sin, which he considers as both the cause of the unfathomable depth of the human problem and the root of the stubbornness and egoism which prevent finding a solution.

There is a change of emphasis in some of Niebuhr's later work, in which he acknowledges that the symbols of Fall and Original Sin are unintelligible to the contemporary mind, and hence begins to emphasize the language and thought patterns of some empirical disciplines such as psychology.[29] However, he seems to have remained committed to the task of chastening the overly optimistic notions of man that emanate from liberal humanism. To do so he creatively rethought and reformulated the Reformation tradition which emphasizes God's revelation and Christ's reconciling activity. In so doing he provides us with a sample of Christian ethics which takes the justification symbol most seriously, focuses attention on man's troubled condition, and offers norms suited to remedying this situation. At the same time, however, he demonstrates how this tradition in Christian ethics can be creatively reworked, giving greater place to humanistic themes such as freedom, human possibilities, and realism in the solution of social and political problems.

Those who prefer the sanctification symbol.   As a general category embracing such differing views as those of Aquinas and Wesley, we should expect sanctificationists to have divergent views on the matter of human nature. Such there are, and some of these will be enumerated. But, as a general category, it is accurate to say that these different views have at least this in common, namely that they all assume a view of man as capable of significant transformation through the work of Christ's sanctifying Spirit. They differ on the degrees and means of this process, but are unanimous in their insistence that something happens to man interiorly, in his subjective states.

The supporters of the sanctification system do not deny the creation-fall-redemption relations of man to God. They simply blur this aspect in highlighting as they do, the effects of the new life of grace within man's spirit. They generally assume the body-spirit dichotomy, the inner-outer split between states and behavior, and lay great stress on the weakened or sinful condition of the man without grace.

The emphasis is on conversion, first of all, so man may leave the sinful life behind and be reborn, becoming a new creature, with new capabilities which transform him interiorly. Secondly, sanctificationists stress the importance of cooperating with this inner force by allowing it to do its work as well as collaborating with it by various practices of self-discipline. The heart of this position then, is found in the basic point of what's happening to man. Having said that all supporters of this system say "he's being sanctified," we must now note how they interpret this process in slightly different ways.

In the works of John Wesley,[30] and in those of many of his Methodist
followers, what happens to man the sinner is a change of will, intention,
and heart. Convinced that all of man's actions are but expressions of his
will, desire and intention, Wesley insisted that the focus be placed on motives
and purposes rather than on outward behavior. Being saved, he believed,
meant being freed from sins of desire and intent. Accordingly, the work of
the Spirit of Christ is one of bringing the roots of human action under its
power and discipline. Such a focus necessarily distracts our attention from
God by a very intensive scrutiny of man, and sets the stage for a set of principles which emphasize openness to the Spirit, supported by disciplined piety.
Ethical norms are heavily weighted in favor of the practice of seeking perfection through the power of the Spirit, making it at least difficult to enter
the everyday world with guidelines which are really adequate for social and
political tasks. There can be no doubt, however, that the Wesleyan interpretation of man is functionally coherent with the understanding of process
and principles put forward in that part of the Christian tradition preferring
the sanctification symbol of what is happening in the Christian life.

In contrast to the Wesleyan tradition, we can identify a line of Catholic
theologians in the tradition of Thomas Aquinas, who interpreted man's
sanctification in a different manner. While this tradition fits in the same
general category as the Wesleyan group, its nuanced handling of the effects
of grace are sufficiently different to warrant a special treatment.

The Thomist tradition is the one from which most contemporary Catholic theologians draw inspiration for their renewal of the doctrine of man. In
this tradition man is understood in relation to his end (that is, the ultimate
end of beatitude with God), and is evaluated as good or evil in terms of how
he tends toward his end. This view of man understands the original condition of man as one in which he had integrity and tended toward his end
naturally. Through the sinful action of his first parents, however, this condition was lost and man tended away from his end. Thus, redemption is interpreted as a rectification of man's natural tendency through a transformation
of his powers which now direct him to a still more glorious and *super*natural
destiny.

The principal difference of this position from that of Wesley is the way
in which this redirection and transformation is understood. Like Wesley,
Aquinas and his school attribute the transforming power to the Spirit of
Christ, who becomes a new law working in men's hearts. But, unique to
Thomists, is the elaborate pattern of virtues by which this general force
extends itself through the various faculties of man. In the Thomist scheme,
man is elevated to new capacity by *theological virtues* (faith, hope, and charity),
but also more proximately transformed by *intellectual virtues*, chief among
which is prudence, and *moral virtues*, crowned by justice. Finally, not only
does the scheme include these fairly permanent habits of mind and heart, it

also elaborates a set of more transient impulses to good action in the momentary promptings called the sevenfold set of "gifts of the Spirit."

Correlative to this scheme, Aquinas and his school affirm the necessity of having vehicles which carry out the work of sanctification. These instruments are, first of all, the Church and its sacraments, and secondly, the various works of piety and behavior suited to both moral and canon (church) law. Out of this conviction arises a series of principles which try to coordinate the norms developed in natural law (what directs man to his natural end), and those arising from positive law, divine and ecclesiastical. Primacy is clearly given to the law of charity, as the "form" of all other virtues, but the scheme of laws is so detailed and intricate that no one can doubt it is a functional result of an equally elaborate understanding of man's nature transformed by grace.[31]

Therefore, while they may differ in detail and rationale, both Wesley and Aquinas give clear witness to the fact that their understanding of people functionally supports the principles they recommend for the Christian.

Those preferring discipleship symbols.　This final grouping of people-views in Christian ethics builds primarily on the assumption that Jesus Christ is the ideal man (the *Urbild*) who is set before us as a model or example (as *Vorbild*). Christian ethicians who prefer discipleship symbols as the organizers of their ethical commentary place most of their emphasis on the imitation of Christ. They may explain this imitative behavior in crassly literal terms of doing the same things Jesus did, or in very subtle and semi-mystical endorsements of putting on the same mind and heart that was in him.

On the whole, theologians who prefer to speak in terms of discipleship have a rather optimistic view of man. This optimism may be due to many different things, among which are two fairly common convictions. On the one hand, many find discipleship thinking most amenable to the optimistic and pragmatic character of American culture. Consequently, this system holds a great appeal for many Americans who share a cultural optimism tied to Jefferson's view of man, and who spurn the pessimism put forth in existentialist and revolutionary expressions coming from Europe. Secondly, many find discipleship thinking most suitable to their doctrinal convictions about man's post-baptismal status. If they are confident that the baptized have been saved, and do not share the justificationists' fears about falling back into sin, then discipleship ethics helps them build constructively on this assurance of salvation.

We can find a rather classical example of this discipleship thinking in the book *In His Steps*, by Charles Sheldon.[32] This work and others like it have enjoyed a wide circulation in the American religious-book market, and have promoted a highly appealing form of popular piety which tries to shape society with Christian principles. However, some of the exponents of discipleship principles have a much more elusive view of man that more closely approximates those detailed in the three preceding sections on Christian ethics. Kierkegaard and Bonhoeffer, Sittler and some Roman Catholics will all be found more closely allied to Lutheran and Thomist models of man. While they use the discipleship symbol frequently in ethical discourse, they assume meanings of man much different than the more popular understanding promoted in ordinary moral discourse in America.

We might note, for example, that Dietrich Bonhoeffer wrote one of his most influential books during the 1930's on the theme of discipleship, but treated this theme with a profundity that is not commonly found in ordinary religious instruction on the imitation of Christ. In fact, in *The Cost of Discipleship*,[33] Bonhoeffer was trying to persuade his fellow Christians in Germany that they had made grace and discipleship appear easy, exchanging justification and righteousness at wholesale prices. His understanding of discipleship was quite different, and one which underscored the cost of grace and the costliness of discipleship. Breaking with the Lutheran tradition which began every serious theological treatise with the Epistle to the Romans, Bonhoeffer began *The Cost of Discipleship* with the paradoxical statements of The Sermon on the Mount, painting a picture of discipleship which made the following of Christ a paradoxical reversal and transformation of human values. From beginning to end he tried to demonstrate that the following of Christ and the witness of the Christian are found more truly in what men consider failure than through the normally accepted criteria of success.

The reader is not, therefore, suprised when he reaches Bonhoeffer's last chapter, "The Image of Christ," and finds there a very profound treatment of both Christ and human nature. In a very brief but brilliant chapter, he opens up some themes which will occupy much of his later theology (the "kenotic Christ" and "Ethics as Formation"),[34] and lays open an understanding of man which distinguishes him sharply from many theologians in the discipleship school of Christian ethics. As Bonhoeffer handles the issue of human nature, it becomes clear that the controlling symbol for man's nature is that of the divine image, which he believes was lost forever through sin. What is required, he claims, is that God take on the form of man, and thereby transform man in his entirety. The really significant thing for Bonhoeffer, then, is not some notion of the form of man or some form of Christ to be followed and imitated; what really counts is the form Christ takes in us.[35]

The treatment of the people factor in Bonhoeffer's ethical thought is very similar to what we have considered in the justification and sanctification symbols of Christian ethics. It demonstrates the uniqueness of Bonhoeffer's thought, and cautions us against categorizing Christian theologians who prefer the discipleship symbolism. They are obviously not the same in every respect, as can be seen in the case of Bonhoeffer, who, at least in the 1930's,[36] preferred to consider ethical questions in terms similar to those who have a much more simplistic view of man, grace, and the imitation of Christ.

The Muslim religious ethic. Building on the revelation of Allah as contained in the Qu'ran, Muslim faith lays great stress on the nature of man as a creature, giving this fact as much a place in thinking about people as do many in the Jewish and Christian traditions. The Correspondence course of the Muslim Student Association quotes the Qu'ran to note that the moral teachings of Islam lean heavily on the characteristic humility and thankfulness which the believer owes to God. For, as Siddiqui reasons, man owes everything to God as his Creator, Who makes and sustains him.[37]

Coupled with this characteristic dependency, however, Islam also underlines man's characteristic responsibility. The believer is not interpreted as one who passively or quietistically receives his salvation from Allah. Rather, man is depicted as the sole subject of his own *falah* (felicity). Instead of passively receiving the gift of a joyous afterlife, man is here portrayed as the only one who can actively create or attain it by virtue of a zealous and active role of responsibility in doing the will of Allah.[38]

In addition, the Muslim faith accentuates the fact that felicity, or happiness, can be sought and attained only *in and through* this world. Both the laws of the Qu'ran and the theological notion of *tawhid* encourage man to take the world seriously and consider life and its activities as a gradual transformation of the world into the content of the divine will and command. Consequently, the other worldly ideal of the saint is generally disvalued in Islam, and, in its place, the ideal of the man zealous about Allah's will in all human affairs is extolled.[39]

In contrast with Christianity and other religions "which burden man's soul with 'original sin' "[40] the Student Course in the Muslim faith makes much of the fact that the Qu'ran teaches otherwise. According to this interpretation, man is born free of guilt with a clean slate, and in *hanif* (good faith, inclining man to monotheistic faith and good deeds). Like the normative strain of the Jewish tradition, Islam seems to prefer "wholistic" thinking about man, refusing to allow rational distinctions between material and spiritual, secular and sacred. Disorder in life is admitted and presupposed in the Qu'ran's teachings which call for the realization of values in life, but this disorder is regarded as a condition of creation as a whole and not the result of any of man's deeds. The ideal of Islam, then, is put forth in terms of the balanced and believing life, which resists placing too much emphasis on any one aspect of human existence, insisting only on a responsible and zealous handling of all human affairs as believers strive to actualize the "ought-to-be" which is the content of the divine will and command.

Throughout the preceding pages of this chapter we have listed a number of examples of how diverse traditions in religious ethics interpret the meaning of man. At times, the functional inter-relationship of this people factor with other factors in the particular ethic was noted. At other times, it was merely inferred for the sake of both treating the particular tradition in its refined nuances and pointing to areas for further study on the part of the reader. In every case, however, I think you will tend to agree with the following statement by Walter Kaufmann: "Every morality is a recipe for a certain type of man, an explication of what man might be."*

STUDY QUESTIONS

1. Compare the writings of Confucius, Mencius and Hsün Tzu. See if you agree with my findings on the changes in their people factor. Are there any corresponding changes in their process factor, in their principles? If their principles remain the same, while the other (two?) factor (s) change, how would you account for this phenomenon?

2. Sample some of the riches and complexity of the Hindu tradition by reading Ainslie T. Embree's *The Hindu Tradition* (New York: The Modern Library, 1966). Try to identify and contrast the nuances in the meanings assigned to people in this tradition. Check your findings to see if the description given in this chapter omits anything significant.

3. How does the people ideal of the Zen Buddhist tradition compare or contrast with the *bodhisattva* ideal of Mahayana Buddhism?

4. Investigate the Jewish interpretation of people as put forward by A. D. Gordon, and found in the summary of Nathan Rotenstreich, *Jewish Philosophy in Modern Times* (New York: Holt, Rinehart and Winston, Inc., 1968).

5. Consider the explanations offered in Karl Barth's *How I Changed My Mind*, with an introduction and epilogue by John D. Godsey, (Richmond: John Knox Press, 1966), later developments in his *Church Dogmatics* and their connection with what he says in *The Humanity of God*. After considering these materials, what would you say is Karl Barth's people factor?

6. Try to identify the Christian tradition from which Jacques Ellul receives his inspiration for an emphasis on the "individual" in works such as *The Technological Society.*

7. Would you say that a significant difference in their people factors helps understand some of the difficulties in finding political solutions between Arabs and Israelis, Indians and Pakistani?

NOTES

1. Cf. B. J. Lonergan, *Insight* (New York: Longmans, Green and Co., 1957).

2. Bruno Bettelheim, "Joey; A 'Mechanical Boy'," in *Scientific American*, **200** : 3 (March, 1959), pp. 116 ff.

* Found in his work *From Shakespeare to Existentialism,* (New York: Doubleday & Company, Inc., 1960), Copyright (C) 1959, 1960 by Walter Kaufmann, p. 217.

3. Cf. Peter Berger, and Thomas Luckmann, *The Social Construction of Reality*, a work to which the comments in this chapter are greatly indebted.

4. Cf. Ernest Becker, "The Evaded Question: Science and Human Nature," in *Commonweal*, **89** : 20 (Feb. 21, 1969), p. 646.

5. Maurice Friedman, *To Deny Our Nothingness*, pp. 17–27, where Friedman gives a clear delineation of what ought to be associated with this phrase.

6. *op. cit.*

7. *Ecclesiasticus* 11 : 1.

8. Cf. *Analects* X : 12 as found in *Sources of Chinese Tradition*, Vol. I, compiled by W. T. de Bary, Wing-Tsit-Chan, and Burton Watson (New York: Columbia University Press, 1960), p. 20.

9. Cf. *Hsün Tzu (Basic Writings)*, trans. by Burton Watson (New York: Columbia University Press, 1963), p. 58.

10. *op. cit.*, p. 160 (and Sect. 19, discussion of rites, p. 89 ff).

11. Cf. *Sources of Chinese Tradition*, Vol. I, pp. 491–502, esp. p. 492.

12. *op. cit.*, pp. 517, 520.

13. Cf. John B. Noss, *Man's Religions* (New York: The Macmillan Company, 1969), p. 288 ff.

14. Cf. *Sources of Chinese Tradition*, Vol. I, p. 85.

15. Jacob B. Agus, "Jewish Ethics," in *Dictionary of Christian Ethics*, ed. John Macquarrie, Philadelphia: Westminster, 1967. pp. 177–80. Cf. also Robert Gordis, "Rejudaizing Christianity," in *The Center Magazine*, I: 6 (September, 1968), pp. 7–16, esp. p. 12.

16. Borowitz, *A New Jewish Theology in the Making*, Chap. 4.

17. *op. cit.*, Chap. 5.

18. *op. cit.*, Chap. 6.

19. Cf. his *The Insecurity of Freedom* (New York: Farrar, Straus, and Giroux, Inc., 1966), Chap. 10 "Sacred Image of Man," pp. 150–67.

20. *op. cit.*, p. 161.

21. Borowitz, *op. cit.*, pp. 160–73.

22. Robert Gordis, *op. cit.*, *loc. cit.*

23. Cf. Karl Barth, *Church Dogmatics* II : 2, G. W. Bromiley and T. F. Torrance, eds. (Edinburgh: T. & T. Clark, 1957), pp. 509–42.

24. Reinhold Niebuhr, *The Nature and Destiny of Man*; Volume I: Human Nature (New York: Charles Scribner's Sons, 1943), p. 160.

25. *op. cit.*, p. 300.

26. *op. cit.*, p. 150.

27. *op. cit.*, Chap. VI, pp. 167–77.

28. op. cit., Chap. VII to IX, pp. 178–264.

29. Cf. his *Man's Nature and His Communities* (New York: Charles Scribner's Sons, 1965), pp. 23–24, 109.

30. Cf. John Wesley, *Christian Perfection*, ed. T. Kepler, Cleveland, 1954. Cf. also

The Standard Sermons of John Wesley, 2 vols., ed. E. H. Sugden, London, 1921, and *The Works of John Wesley*, cf. in readex microprint edition of Early American Imprints, published by American Antiquities Society.

31. G. Gilleman, *The Primacy of Charity in Moral Theology* (Westminster, Md.: Newman Press, 1959).

32. Charles Sheldon, *In His Steps*, 1896 cf. its "grandchild" in Glenn Clark's, *What Would Jesus Do?* (St. Paul: Macalester, 1946).

33. New York: The Macmillan Company, 1963.

34. Cf. his *Ethics* (New York: The Macmillan Company, 1965), pp. 64–119, esp. 80–85.

35. *The Cost of Discipleship*, Sect. 32, p. 337 ff.

36. It is clear from his *Ethics* and *Letters and Papers from Prison* that he was uncertain which set of symbols he should allow the dominant role in his ethical writings. Justification, Formation and Responsibility play important roles in these works, with indications of Bonhoeffer's uncertainty about which one should be central.

37. M. Moinuddin Siddiqui, *Islamic Correspondence Course*, Unit 8: "Moral Teachings of Islam," p. 2; cf. also texts of Qu'ran in *The Great Asian Religions*, pp. 347–48.

38. Isma'īl Rāgī al Fārūqī, "Islam" in *The Great Asian Religions*, p. 316.

39. *ibid.*; Cf. also texts of Qu'ran in *ibid.*, pp. 349 ff.

40. Siddiqui, *op. cit.*, p. 3; cf. also texts of Qu'ran in *ibid*, pp. 349 ff.

chapter four

Principles

ANY TREATMENT OF THE TOPIC of this chapter requires of both the writer and the reader a great deal of balance and good judgment. For, wherever ethics has been or will be discussed, the principles factor plays a prominent, often exclusive, role. In fact, the outer appearances of social groups, including religions, are known primarily by their behavior and the rationale (principles!) they allege as the justification for it. Some body of guidelines, varying from the merely suggestive to the more binding prescriptive, lies behind every institutionalized set of behaviors, and can even be discovered behind the activities of idiosyncratic individuals, if only in so simple a rule as "do your own thing!"

Consequently, balanced judgments are required of one who would understand this ubiquitous factor, which lies behind the conscious behavior of both individuals and groups. Moreover, a thoughtful discussion of principles is a requisite laid down by virtue of the elaborate and extensive changes in social behavior in the "new industrial state," changes which have been paralleled by equally impressive debates on the principles by which we guide and evaluate our activities in this new milieu. We therefore bear both the fruit and the burden of these discussions in any contemporary treatment of principles.

When dealing with this factor we must also be alert to developments in philosophical analysis of the language of moral discourse, as well as to the critical studies of traditional norms and the stances they manifest in answer to the question "why be moral?" Consequently, our discussion of principles will have to take account of both their wide popularity and the more recent clarifications brought to light about their meaning and use. Hence, it seems fitting to alert the reader to the fact that what follows will not only attempt an accurate statement of this factor but will also invite suggestions for further accuracy and clarity from whomever finds it needed.

The Meaning
of the Principles Factor

In the preceding chapter I called for a convention on the meaning of the people factor, asking that we let it equal whatever men understand themselves to be or intend to be. Once again, in this chapter, I would ask that we come to a preliminary agreement on the meaning of the principles factor. Let "principles" stand for any concrete and communicable statement of a value to be achieved in behavior. It can include the popular subculture imperative "make love not war" as well as the formal legal requirements of "trial by jury" and specifically religious commands like "remember to keep holy the sabbath."

Some principles[1] can be more general or universal while still qualifying as concrete and communicable statements of a value to be achieved. The general advice about "considering the consequences of your action" is one such principle. It recommends something specific and concrete, namely careful consideration, but yet is general enough not to require highly particularized forms of consideration. It has value only to the extent that people apply the rule, but is communicable enough to convey a message about how to behave when making a decision.

The extensive and illuminating debates about principles in this century both provide and demand further precision in our present discussion. Hence, we ought to further clarify the meaning of principles with a brief look at the various levels of moral discourse from which ethical statements arise. This will elucidate both the kind of language employed in principles and the context in which they are used. For example, we can follow the analysis of moral discourse given by H. D. Aiken in his book *Reason and Conduct*, where he isolates at least four distinct levels on which the language of morality ("good, right, ought") is employed.* He calls these the (1) expressive-evocative level, (2) the moral level, (3) the ethical level, and (4) the post-ethical or human level. These levels are isolated and distinguished by virtue of the different contexts in which moral discourse occurs.

On the *expressive-evocative* level, language is of the unreflective variety, expressing feelings of spontaneous pleasure or displeasure ("Hurrah" or "Groan"). It should be noted, contends Aiken, that the language on this

* The following is a synopsis of Henry David Aiken's *Reason and Conduct* (New York: Alfred A. Knopf, Inc., 1962), pp. 65–87, Copyright (c) 1962 by Henry David Aiken, with permission of Alfred A. Knopf, Inc.

level is not really questionable or debatable, but does, nevertheless, contain a seed of the cognitive and has a rhetorical or incitive quality in its effects upon those who witness or interpret it.

The *moral* level is the one that most interests us in our study of principles. For it is here that reflective questions arise, asking what one ought to do and inquiring about the relevance of certain criteria (principles!) for deciding what is good, right, or obligatory. Usually, reflections on this level focus on both factual appraisals of the situation and give attention to rules and procedures which may guide decision and action.

The language on this level issues from a context of decision-making, the area of moral study which is usually given the most attention. The language reveals personal efforts to justify or give reasons for one's decisions and behavior. It is decidedly practical language, composed of very concrete and communicable statements of what is to be achieved or realized in behavior. On this level we generally resort to acquired habits of evaluation and employ certain key rules as our primary guidelines.

Some examples of such primary guidelines were given to me by a group of students a few years ago and tell us a great deal about the kinds of guidelines we actually utilize. Out of a group of about twenty students only half responded to the question "how were you taught to make decisions?" and a follow-up question "what procedures were recommended to you?" The first six who responded gave answers having little or nothing to do with religious standards and offered the following primary principles of decision-making.

> 1. Think of what will enable you to hold your head up high: Think it through and consider the opinion others may have of you only secondarily.
> 2. As long as you don't get caught, whatever you do will be all right.
> 3. Consider the problem and the consequences of your decision, and do the least harmful thing.
> 4. Size up the situation intuitively and act.
> 5. Be honest in your decisions and whatever you do will be correct.
> 6. Be virtuous in your behavior and, if you are not, you will be punished.

The second group offering an answer to the same questions said they were taught to:

> 1. Have a God-directed conscience and do the unselfish thing.
> 2. Pray and the solution will come to you.
> 3. Do what won't embarrass Christ.
> 4. Talk to the minister, counsellor, or some moral authority about it.

Ethicians and moral counsellors will consider most of these statements imperfect at best, if not totally erroneous, and will suggest more "human, rational, religious" guidelines. However, in mentioning the above rules, my purpose is to exemplify what was *actually* operative in the language of these ten students. While the sampling is extremely limited and given in a cultural context of the southwestern United States, it demonstrates the kind of principles that come readily to the fore in response to the kind of questions I asked. The responses are open to debate, require improvements, but do, nevertheless, exemplify the kind of moral principles that are consciously used by some people, thus providing us with *prima facie* examples of moral discourse on the moral level.

On the *ethical* level of moral discourse critical questions arise about the principles actually used on the moral level. The effort here is one of testing the validity of these principles, attempting to evaluate them in an impersonal ("unbiased" and "scientific") manner. In ethical questions we are asked to consider whether or not we ought to alter our set of rules, whether or not they cover all eventualities, *et cetera*. On this level, it is no longer a case of simply justifying our actions by reference to our principles; the principles themselves must also be justified. Few people have the time or inclination to engage in this discussion. Hence, it is generally limited to academic studies in ethics, or relegated to professional ethicians in their journals and conferences. Since they have no immediate utility for people making decisions, the principles developed in discussions on the ethical level are generally not utilized in the moral instruction suggested to ordinary men making decisions in ordinary situations. We will find, therefore, that teachers of religious ethics make less use of these kinds of principles in statements to their faithful, and tend to concentrate on the formulation of principles and rules proper to the moral level of the language of behavior.

The fourth distinctive level, the *post-ethical* or *human* level, uses language proper to the context of one's stand or perspective in life. The questions posed are variations of the single question "why be moral?" The answers given are not so much explanations as they are statements of fact indicating a commitment. The commitment may be simply that of being human, or it may be some other motivation such as being a good Buddhist or Muslim. There is no one possible answer, and no single criterion for evaluating the answers given. What is said in response is usually a bald statement of the fact that a person has adequate motivation for "playing the moral game."

The fourth level may also be discussed in terms of its dependence on still other factors, for one's ethical stance is functionally related to one's self-understanding and the kind of process in which he operates. Hence, more than anywhere else, the functional tie between the three factors becomes most cogently clear. Even if ethicians and morally-minded persons do not often mention the inter-relationship of these three factors, the connections should still be noted. On the post-ethical level of discourse, people begin to tell us what they understand about themselves and the theater in which they act. They reveal a stance or perspective which justifies their commitments to certain principles in preference to others, and thereby evidence the functional connection between process-people-principles.

The foregoing distinction of levels of moral language should clarify our discussion of the principles factor in at least two ways. First of all, it points out that what we are primarily concerned with in this chapter are the statements made on the second, or moral level, of discourse.[2] Secondly, it indicates a way in which we might interpret the tacit and not always manifest ties between factors on the post-ethical level.

How Religious Interpretation
Helps Shape Principles

It is commonly said that every human culture has some form of religious influence providing commitment and an answer to the post-ethical question "why be moral?" The motivation to be moral, to act out of principles, and to be concerned about justifying one's behavior arises from the stance and perspective provided by diverse religious traditions. The cohesiveness given to culture by religion was noted in a recent angered statement of an American revolutionary who claimed that "religion is the glue in the spit of the establishment." Putting it more moderately he might have observed that it seems true to say that religion often provides a view of life's process and an interpretation of what man is and ought to be. It thereby provides a platform of beliefs and values which transcend ordinary questions and challenges, one which easily, and unquestionably, moves to concrete and communicable statements of values to be achieved in behavior. Since the post-ethical stance is often impervious to criticism, the first principles emanating from it exhibit an unassailability which provides endless frustrations for critics of plans and procedures relying on these principles.

There is yet another, more easily observable way in which religion helps shape what we encounter in principles. When focusing attention on the second level of moral discourse we observed that this level carries the burden of our statements of what is right or obligatory. The set of rules by which individuals and communities shape their decisions is often influenced by religious thought. Our task, therefore, is to identify some of the ways in which this occurs.

By originating. First of all, it can be said that religious people are responsible for originating some of the common maxims of moral discourse. Confucius gave his civilization some very specific sayings, as did the Buddha, and both continue to influence the decision-making of large segments of the world's population, at least through the maxims they have developed. The moral statements of the Bible, most frequently given divine authority if not authorship, are still used by many in the western hemisphere either to guide or to justify their decisions and actions.

Many interesting questions can be raised about the ultimate source of these norms which are here considered to be of religious origin. Social and cultural studies give rise to several variant theories about the origin of such teachings, questioning the originality of religious authors and pointing to purely secular sources from which these religionists may have borrowed their principles. It seems inappropriate to raise these questions in this present context since they will introduce many nearly insoluble problems which would distract from our immediate concerns. Therefore, we will temporarily invoke the common judgment of men that certain religions have originated, either on their own or as "spokesmen for god(s)," some widely influential rules for deciding and behaving.

By extending. Religious traditions have not always contented themselves with instructing only their faithful adherents. They have, at times, extended their influence by providing assistance to social and political institutions, proposing moral norms to be used in the construction of principles of socio-political or legal varieties. This is especially true of those religious traditions where there is a conviction that their set of principles is "the one, true pattern," given by God with a mandate to make them known, if not adopted, by the general public and its institutional leaders.

This zealous attitude has frequently led to conflicts over civil legislation and public life. It plays a part in some recent conflicts in Northern Ireland, as well as the on-going debates between Hindus and Muslims in both India and Pakistan. Japan also has experienced tension in its Parliament as a result of the zeal of militant Soka Gakkai Buddhists. Christianity, more than Judaism, has a long history of propagandizing its moral principles. It has been most zealous about social laws and practices, not only in cultures where Christians were in the majority, but in others as well, where Christians were both religious aliens and ethnic foreigners to the people being evangelized.

Through efforts such as these the principles originating in particular religions have been extended in scope, frequently being adopted by people who are not members of the evangelizing religious group, and occasionally being institutionalized in the form of social and political laws or customs. In the latter case religious moral norms enjoy a continuing influence and are extended in time by the socialization process passing on customs and maxims from generation to generation.

By reinforcing. Not all moral principles of social groups are religious in origin nor are all religious principles from an exclusively sacred source. The interplay between the religious insight and other human judgments must be acknowledged in the area of moral norms. Religions frequently endorse or reinforce the human judgments of people competent in special areas of behavior. They may merely ratify "good medicine" as "good religious conduct," or lend support to social judgments about the programs needed to alleviate poverty. Frequently too, religions take the insights and recommendations of psychologists and sociologists and give them the stamp of divine approbation. In this manner religions often support the principles arising from "secular" sources, inspire confidence in them for large numbers of people, and thereby reinforce the norms by "throwing the weight" of religion behind them.

We conclude, therefore, that religion helps shape the principles which are actually used in people's decision-making. In some instances it may be in the form of giving birth to some meaningful norms to guide members' choices and conduct. In other cases it may be by extending the knowledge of these guidelines to others searching for assistance, or even by exerting political pressure to have them institutionalized. Finally, there are times when religion shapes principles by either adopting or adding motivation to the use of moral rules coming from whatever area of human judgment which accurately formulates what is good, right, or obligatory.

Principles as One of the
Functioning Factors in Religious Ethics

In order to consider "principles" as a single unified factor in a religious ethic it is necessary to consider all the principles of a particular ethic as a single "set." Thus, an entire set of principles will be taken as a unit and viewed as a single factor functioning interrelatedly with the people and process factors.

The principal goal of this chapter will be one of demonstrating the functional ties between the principles factor and other factors already studied. We will be attempting to point out the ways in which a set of principles both affects and is affected by the positions taken on process and people. We could also study the interactions between principles *within* a given set, such as the coherence between principles of business and those of medicine. This would give further evidence of the attempts at consistency those elaborating principles, but would extend this study far beyond reasonable limits. Hence, contenting ourselves with a mere suggestion of this possible area of study, we will limit our investigation to a treatment of sets of principles taken as wholes, and viewed in their functional ties to the other key factors in religious ethics.

However, before demonstrating this inter-connection a word of caution is in order. We must be careful not to consider the principles factor as the least important one simply because it is dealt with in the series of factors. Quite to the contrary, it can be, and often is, the *most* important and influential factor of the three. A set of principles is much more proximately bound to actual behavior than are the more general factors of process and people. Principles come up for questioning more readily than the other factors because they are the judgments most immediately responsible for our decisions and actions. Consequently, if these proximate norms of everyday activity are out of tune with the facts of our present experience they become problematic and call for revision. A classic instance of this is found in the challenging of the "just war" principles in the light of the facts and experiences of the nuclear age.

Principles are more often discussed than are worldviews and anthropologies. They are always in a greater state of flux than are the other factors, and principles will frequently change before we have a chance to modify our views of man and the world process. For this reason, then, changing principles very often place the first strain on the coherence of ethical systems, and are thereby responsible for the rethinking and reworking of the two other factors. For example, principles revamped to fit life in the industrial age soon place a strain on older agricultural models of man and history necessitating a terribly difficult but necessary reconstruction of many religious ethical systems in western societies.

Although we deal with the principles factor last in our order of study, we acknowledge the fact that it may be the first consideration in the actual or chronological order of influence. However, this need not impugn the order in which we are treating these factors, for functional ties can be touched anywhere along the system and lead eventually to all other important factors in the system. When talking about them apart from their actual operations, then, we may proceed in the order that best suits the kind of understanding we want. And this has been the guiding criterion for this study, dealing with process-people-principles in that order, while acknowledging that, in actual practice, any one of these can become the fundamental building block for a particular religious ethic.

With this forewarning in mind, we now turn to an examination of the sets of principles used in the ethical systems of the religious traditions which we have been using as examples in the two preceding chapters. In considering these sets of principles our principal concern will be to understand if and how they are functionally related to the views of process and people in each of the religious systems under scrutiny. Once again, for the sake of clarity and continuity, we will use examples in two broad categories of religious ethics, those holding a cyclical worldview and those belonging to the linear view of world process.

THE CYCLICAL PERSPECTIVE

Confucianism. The ethics of Confucius is sometimes referred to as an "optimistic humanism," based as it is on a hopeful view about the reformability of both man and his society. While it is important to recall this fact when dealing with Confucianism, we should also note that Confucius had a great deal more to say about detailed rules and principles than he did about human nature. As noted in the preceding chapter, Mencius and Hsün Tzu devoted a great deal of time to a discussion of basic human goodness, but followed the leading of Confucius in making norms the bulk of their discussion.

The question before us is whether or not the principles enunciated in the five virtues and relationships are systematically inter-related to Confucius' understanding of people and the process in which they find themselves. In order to answer this question we must first examine the five virtues, and secondly, the five relationships. It seems that Confucius had arrived at the conclusion that his society was deteriorating because people did not have the will to work for the good of others. Hence, he elaborated a set of virtues necessary for securing the common good by using a metaphor of a fruit-bearing tree. Its root is the will to work for others (*jen*); its trunk is justice (*ji*); the branches are religious or moral ways of acting (*li*); its flower is wisdom (*chih*); and its fruit faithfulness (*hsin*).[3]

Of these five virtues *li* is the one most frequently appearing in his works, and Confucius himself said to Duke Ai that ". . . of all the things people live by, *li* is the greatest."* Yet *li* is also the most indefinable of the virtues and is applied to diverse things in different contexts, indicating that it means something like the axiom "everything in its place." In historical context, however, *li* probably meant everything in its proper, rational, and *feudal* place.[4] Nevertheless, it is also the virtue in which we can definitely see a tie to Confucius' process factor (the *Tao*) for, as he himself noted, "this *li* is the principle by which the ancient kings *embodied the laws of heaven and regulated the expressions of human nature.*"† *Li* regulates home, village, and empire, bringing about the goal of universal process, namely, cosmic harmony between men, the earth, and the heavens.

In the scheme of Confucius the expressions of human nature are indeed multiple, but can be reduced to five main relationships. These are the ties between ruler and subject, father and son, husband and wife, the oldest son and his younger brothers, elders and juniors. Confucius mentions other relationships as well but considers the above five as the most basic ones, the so-called "great relationships." These reciprocal ties are further clarified by the Confucian detail of the "proper" attitudes to be maintained in these basic relations. The father's attitude is to be one of kindness and the son's one of filial piety. Rulers are to be benevolent and subjects reciprocally loyal. Husbands ought to be righteous in their behavior, and wives obedient. The conduct of the eldest brother should be characteristically gentle, while the

* Lin Yutang, *The Wisdom of Confucius*, (New York: Random House, Inc., 1938), p. 216. Copyright 1938 by Random House, Inc. (Note: Italics mine).
† Yutang, *The Wisdom of Confucius*, p. 216.

younger ones are to behave with respect and humility toward the "number one son." The older members of a society are worthy of deference from its junior members, who, in turn, must be given humane consideration by the elders.

If these attitudes are actually observed then society will possess *li*, and perfect harmony (*tao*) will preside, giving harmony in the home, peace in the state, and happiness among friends. The rules of social order are, however, futile if man does not have the will to work for the good of others. Hence, while *li* represents the branches of the Confucian tree of behavior, this tree must also have a root which is *jen*. This foundational virtue must be cultivated even more earnestly than *li*, for, without a recognition of the worth of others, or without a willingness to behave kindly toward them, no set of principles can bring the peace and harmony aimed at by *li* and the rules of social relationships.

In the coupling of *li* and *jen* supporting Confucius' principles we have ample evidence of the functional tie between the factors in his system. *Li* presupposes the traditional view of a harmonious universe, and *jen* both assumes and encourages an optimistic view of man. Without these two related factors none of the rules in Confucius' set of principles would make sense.

Before dealing with Taoist moral principles we should mention one of the characteristic differences between oriental and western ethical systems. Both the Confucian and Taoist sets of principles are quite different from those common to westerners. There are indeed points of coincidence between eastern and western moral principles and the virtues they uphold. Yet, eastern principles are characteristically paradoxical, following a tradition of wisdom that defies translation into western logic. This difficulty is less obvious in the principles of Confucius than in those of Taoism. The latter system, as we shall see, communicates most of its moral principles in very poetic, and often mystical, statements by sages who never valued codes or law books composed out of a desire for logical coherence and consistency.

The ethics of both traditions do, however, have the kind of systematic coherence which is proper to a "good story" (cf. chapter I), and both make concrete and communicable statements of values to be achieved in human behavior. Hence, Confucianism and Taoism are systematic in the sense defined earlier, and both have an identifiable "principles" factor in their systems.

Taoism. Taoism is extremely problematic when it comes to the matter of defining which particular part of the Taoist tradition you have in mind. Not only is the legend of Lao-tzu historically questionable, but there is also a question about how much, if any, of the *Tao-te-ching* is actually his work. Furthermore, Taoism can be divided into several phases, all of which are quite different in their teaching. For example, we can talk about its formative phase (5th to 4th centuries B.C.), its magical phase (3rd to 1st centuries B.C.) and its official state-religion phase (A.D., esp. from the 11 th c. on).[5]

In this study we have concentrated on its formative stage, the period in which Lao-tzu's teachings were given coherent form. This is also the period in which the *Tao-te-ching* seems to have been revised, edited, and finalized, as well as the time in which Chuang-tzu elaborated his philosophy.

The short cryptic sentences of the *Tao-te-ching* have much to say about proper behavior. They are in sharp contrast to the orderly and disciplined arrangements of Confucius' teachings, and communicate a very different kind of advice about behavior. Over and again they recommend a style of natural and spontaneous behavior that lets things take their course. For example, the advice given to government is to follow a style of *laissez-faire*, practicing non-interference in the lives of citizens. This is recommended in the sayings of Lao-tzu as the only true path to freedom and peace, the longed-for qualities of every harmonious society.[6] The *Tao-te-ching* repeatedly endorses the virtue of *wu-wei*, that is, the practice of nonaggression, or non-meddlesome action. Positively stated, the principles embodied in the sayings of Lao-tzu advise one to cooperate with the *tao*, to produce and not to possess, to act but not to assert one's self, to develop life but not to dominate it. Stated negatively, these recommendations can be summed up in the advice that says "don't meddle with nature."

Taken as a whole these sayings are quite consistent with each other, and are coherently related to other sayings which formulate the Taoist view of process and people. The *Tao-te-ching* is functionally systematic in formulating the belief that when things are allowed to take their natural course they move in perfect harmony with the way of the *Tao*. Man can disrupt this harmony by setting up his own plans and being too aggressive, but he is wise and happy only if he stops fighting with nature and cooperates with its inner harmonious law of effortlessness.

The same holds true for the Taoism elaborated by Chuang-tzu (4th c. B.C.) one of this tradition's most philosophical writers. He too placed the *tao* principle of harmony in a central position, but viewed its process as a series of transformations. He thought that time moved in a circular pattern, and that the seasons mutually produced and destroyed each other. The male and female principles, *yang* and *yin*, spring from the *Tao* and they too operate on the norm of reciprocal causality. We have attractions and repulsions, loves and hates, peace and danger, all in reciprocal cycles. Therefore, there is no set way of behaving, no standard to which we can conform. The wise man knows this and submits to it. He doesn't argue about right and wrong, large and small, high and low, but simply lets the transforming cycles of *Tao* happen. By so doing he is truly himself (the *people* factor), and helps blend everything into a harmonious whole (the *process* factor), but only if he lets things be (the *principles* factor).

Hinduism-Buddhism. From its Indian inception with Siddartha Gautama (6th c. B.C.), Buddhism has shown a strong proclivity for the creation of practical principles of behavior. This original Buddha ("enlightened one") went through stages of realization which brought him to the conclusion that suffering and rebirth—Hindu themes—were caused by craving and ignorance of life's illusory character. He reasoned that men could be liberated from life's pain and achieve enlightenment by harnessing their physical and mental powers through *yoga* practices. In this way, men would be able to climb the steps of meditation to arrive at *satori*, the enlightenment experience. This was the heart of his first sermon at Benares, where he concluded that the way to achieve *satori* was the route he called "The Eightfold Path."[7]

When he elaborated the steps to *nirvana*, the Buddha was operating on the basis of the ancient Indian understanding of world process. This view claimed that everything operates according to eternal and cosmic moral laws, which are manifested in *dharmas*, present in a person as definite laws of feeling, perception, moral relationships, and consciousness. If you can discover these laws and cooperate with them, then you have found the "chain of causation" which links past, present, and future lives all in one. This was the Buddha's claim and preaching effort, as he tried to teach men the principles by which they too could destroy the unhappiness of life, discover the "chain" and bring the endless cycle of rebirths to a halt.[8]

The Buddha taught his followers a set of principles called the eightfold path. Herein he set out a path of doing what is right in:

1. understanding
2. purpose
3. speech
4. conduct
5. vocation
6. effort
7. alertness
8. concentration[9]

He reinforced steps three to five in this path with a set of five precepts. These precepts, however negative in form, instruct the Buddhist more concretely than do the general principles of the path. They forbid murder, stealing, fornication and adultery, lying and gossiping, and the use of consciousness-reducing drugs and liquor. These five precepts apply to monks and layman alike, but are buttressed with additional norms for the monks (poverty, celibacy, and self-mortification). As can readily be seen, they are quite simple in form, and, therefore, leave considerable room for expansion by later Buddhists of the Mahayana school.[10]

Before treating the specific additions of Mahayana Buddhism, we should note the systematic coherence between the principles of early Buddhism and its understanding of people and the processes of the world. Cosmic laws of process were understood to be manifested in the *dharmas* that make up people. One (primarily the *arhat*, or monk) discovers these *dharmas* and works out his salvation (a cessation of rebirth and suffering) by following the principles outlined in the eightfold path and its accompanying precepts. However, this functional inter-relationship is challenged by subsequent developments in Mahayana Buddhism, which fashions several transformations of the original "story."

As earlier noted, Buddhism entered a devotional phase beginning in the third century B.C., corresponding to its time of greatest missionary endeavor, and leading to a considerably expanded version of the earlier, almost exclusively monastic form, of Theravadan Buddhism. Mahayana, or "larger-vehicle" Buddhism had a richer life of ritual and worship, a new emphasis on the Bodhisattva ideal of a compassionate "mediator," and a new set of principles promoting the more active (vs. monastic) style of life. Only later, in the second century A.D., did Buddhism substantially change its view of world process. This was accomplished by Nagarjuna during a period of keen philosophical interest in the traditional teaching about the "chain of causation." This change in the process factor seems to be connected with centuries of experienced changes in the people and principles factors. Mahayana Buddhism had long extolled a new ideal of the compassionate and socially-concerned man, and had created norms suited to it. Only centuries later did it work out a revision of the old process view bringing it too into harmony with the other two factors.

Furthermore, when Mahayana Buddhism extolled the Bodhisattva ideal, it soon became clear that the old set of principles suited to the monastic ideal were inadequate. Consequently, to the eightfold path and the five precepts, the Mahayana school added ten perfections (*paramitas*). These *paramitas*, or cardinal virtues, enjoin upon a Buddha-to-be the practices of generosity, discipline, patience, energy, meditation, perception, skill in sharing truth, determination, knowledge, and wonder-working.[11]

The addition of these typically compassionate principles puts a strain on the more individualistic principles of traditional Buddhism. A similar pressure is evidenced in the people factor changing from the socially-separated *arhat* to that of the socially-involved *Bodhisattva*. Centuries later, these two tensions brought about a similar strain on the accepted interpretation of world process, and efforts were made to bring the system into some kind of equilibrium. Theravadan Buddhism continued on its customary path but Mahayana Buddhism inherited the old system, its developmental tensions, and the task of working out a coherent story. This it did, and it seems that it did so by attending to the functional interrelationships of the three key factors.

THE LINEAR PERSPECTIVE

The religious systems with a linear view of process are rooted in the experience and insight of the Near East. With few exceptions they generally place a high premium on human individuality and put great stress on the moral element in man-to-God, and man-to-man relationships. One of the most common questions in systems as different as Zoroastrianism and Christianity, Judaism and Islam, is one which asks "What does God want me to do?" or "What is His will for me?" The answers given are statements of moral rules, ranging from highly prescriptive and detailed legal codes to more broadly stated guidelines recommending general attitudes such as love.

Our concern at this point is to present a representative sampling of various subsystems of the ethical traditions of Judaism, Christianity, and Islam. Hence, as in the preceding chapters, we shall consider the application of the systems analogy to (1) post-Kantian Jewish ethics, (2) post-reformation Christian ethics, and (3) The Muslim religious ethic.

Post-Kantian Jewish ethics. There can be no doubt about the centrality of the principles factor in the Jewish tradition. If principles may be realized in behavior, then the *Torah* and *Talmud* of Judaism have surely attempted it. Admittedly, Jewish thinkers disagree on the relative importance of various sets of laws, distinguishing among them the moral law, the ceremonial laws, dietary laws, etc. Furthermore, they also disagree on the source(s) of these various laws, as Eugene Borowitz notes in the following quotation: "Jewish law is God-given to Heschel, folk created in different ways to Baeck and Kaplan, and man-created out of dialogue with God to Buber."*

Yet, despite these differences, moral principles hold so prominent a place in all of Judaism that one generally hears more about Jewish laws than about the Jewish understanding of God, man, and history. Consequently, even if we had no other reason for treating process and people earlier in this study, it was valuable to have considered the importance and function of these factors before allowing ourselves to become totally preoccupied with the very elaborate principles factor of Judaism.

In considering the function of the principles factor in Jewish ethics we will be using the same examples chosen for chapters two and three, seen now from the vantage point of the way they handle moral principles.

COHEN AND BAECK—
"KANT AND BEYOND"

The nineteenth-century thought of Hermann Cohen is decidedly Kantian, with primacy given to ethics, interpreting the essence of Judaism as ethical monotheism. As he and Leo Baeck (in his early work) saw it, Judaism was essentially ethical with its monotheism coming to light primarily as a result of the emphasis on the absolute character of the law.[12] It is debatable whether or not Cohen ever changed his opinion on this matter,

---

* From *A New Jewish Theology in the Making*, by Eugene B. Borowitz. Copyright (c) MCMLXVIII, The Westminster Press. Used by permission.

but there can be no doubt that Baeck did. A definite shift of opinion can be seen between two works of Leo Baeck published over the course of a half century. The earlier position is marked by the publication of *The Essence of Judaism* in 1905, and the later transformed position is manifest in his last publication *This People Israel*, 1955. In both these works we find ample evidence of systematic interrelationships of the three ethical factors. Consequently, Baeck's work will be given the most attention in preference to Cohen's more problematic and disputed positions.

Like Cohen, Baeck's early work arose from an idealist Kantian position with primary emphasis on the ethical imperative. As he himself wrote in that period, "Besides the one flawlessly moral God, there can be no other gods, because the one morality does not tolerate anything contrary to itself."* Everything flows from this "pure concept," building a monotheistic doctrine of God, a universalism of mankind whose future rests with their recognition of the One God and His demands.[13]

To this view of world process, Baeck adds a notion of man optimistically conceived as creative, free and independent, having nobility, and capable of realizing in himself the good which is rooted in God.[14]

Accordingly, his understanding of principles coheres with these other two factors, and, in fact, seems to dominate them, at least in his early work. For example, in *The Essence of Judaism* Baeck highlights Judaism as ethical monotheism, contrasting it with Christian interests in dogmas and creeds, saying:

> Veiled in a dark remoteness which no mortal eye can penetrate, the being of God can be approached by man only through pious behavior and silent meditation. Man's function is described by the commandments: to do what is good; that is the beginning of wisdom. Man's duty toward man comes before his knowledge of God, and the knowledge of him is a process of seeking and inquiring rather than an act of possession. In the Jewish view, God makes certain demands upon man, but these demands are in relation to the life in which he has placed man. The 'principles of the Torah' are therefore, as the Talmud remarks, the principles of pious conduct. These principles are embodied in definite religious forms. . . . Judaism also has its Word, but it is only one word— 'to do'. . . . The deed becomes proof of conviction. Judaism too has its doctrine, but it is a doctrine of behavior, which must be explored in action in order that it may be fulfilled. Hence there is no doctrine in Judaism other than the expression of the divine command.†

---

* Simon Bernfeld, ed., *The Foundations of Jewish Ethics* (New York: KTAV Publishing House, Inc., 1968 rev. ed.), p. 17.

† Reprinted by permission of Schocken Books Inc. from *The Essence of Judaism*, by Leo Baeck. Copyright (c) 1948 by Schocken Books Inc.

Yet man is more than a mere puppet of a divine master; he is creative, free and independent. As Baeck describes this creativity, he emphasizes man's consciousness of "the categorical imperative, of the categorical responsibility,"† demonstrating both his nineteenth-century optimism and his preferences for the philosophy of Immanuel Kant. Furthermore, he clearly manifests his conviction of the primacy of deeds and their guiding principles in his rendition of the place of ethics in Judaism. For "all experience demands action; and for Judaism experience can become religious only through the deed . . . Only in the deed does man's personality gain its content."†

Yet, for Baeck, Jewish ethics is not mere moralism, with ambiguous demands or merely finite clarifications of responsibilities. The principles of Judaism are commandments of God, and, even though Judaism puts the greatest stock in the moral deed and attempts to describe God in moral terms, there is still no ethics without belief in God and formulated as a kind of service to Him.[15]

However, in the words of Albert H. Friedlander, ". . . as the author of *The Essence of Judaism* walked through the dark valley, the idealistic vision of the teachings of Judaism merged with the existential reality of the Jewish people. And a new book emerged . . . *This People Israel* . . . written in the concentration camp . . . ."* Fifty years after the first mentioned work, Baeck now describes man, not as one who approaches God, but as one who is approached by Him and is lifted above himself, becoming creative as if by a miracle.[16] The commandment is born out of mystery, and man becomes aware of himself, not in Kantian terms, but only if he has heard The One behind the commands, and has experienced the aura of majesty residing in the sentences of Sinai or entered into dialogue with the eternal I who directs Himself to man.[17]

There is something new here, identified by some as the intervening influence of Rudolf Otto's *mysterium tremendum* and Martin Buber's personalist existentialism.[18] The process and people factors are transformed, fit to a model of man "the responder," who is not in himself creative but only in relationship to God. Hence, the earlier emphasis on the absolute character of moral principles is likewise tempered and brought into line with these developments. We now find Baeck saying that:

> Ethical monotheism has been a favorite term used to emphasize
> the unique character of the religion of Israel. It is useful, but
> incomplete. There is more to the character of this religion than

---

* *This People Israel* by Leo Baeck. Translated and Introductory Essay by Albert H. Friedlander, (New York: Holt, Rinehart and Winston, Inc., 1964), p. xv. Cf. also p. xviii where Frienlander describes the transition as one ". . . from essence to existence, from nineteenth century optimism to twentieth century existentialism. . . ." (*Note:* the concentration camp referred to is that of Theresienstadt, Germany.)

† See p. 103.

its teaching of the *One* God and His law, more than its monotheism and its ethics. Everything proceeds from the One God;
everything returns to the One God. He is the focus of all that is, and
all that shall be. It is precisely this theocentricity which allows
monotheism to achieve its character and its completeness.*

From testimony such as this we can reasonably conclude that Baeck's
work shows the functional ties of the three factors in religious ethics. Furthermore, we can see how changes in one or more of the key factors provokes
a change in the others. For, as ethical monotheism moved from the position
of defining Judaism's essence to being an incomplete description of it, there
were behind the scenes some important shifts in the meaning of man and the
process in which he encounters God.

KAPLAN AND RECONSTRUCTIONISM

During the thirties and forties Mordecai Kaplan was laying the foundations of American Judaism's youngest movement, Reconstructionism. He
understood Judaism in terms of a "reconstructing people," an evolving
religious civilization which had come through centuries of development.[19]
According to his point of view, religion was one of the essential aspects of
this civilization, but should not be considered co-extensive with it. In fact,
following in the Durkheim tradition of social thought, Kaplan maintained
that a people is necessarily prior to its religion, and that Judaism had created
its own religious dimensions in much the same way it had fashioned the
linguistic, literary, cultural, social and geographical aspects of its civilization.

With the people factor holding center stage in his reflections, Kaplan
looks at the religious principles of Judaism (*Torah*) as "folkways" by which
a people externalize the reality of their collective existence. These folkways
are distinguishable as either religious or cultural according to the interest
around which they center, and not according to their source (divine and
human as in more orthodox Judaism).[20] The principles of the *Torah*, then,
are simply folk-created externalizations of communal life which enable
individuals to effect a creative adjustment to reality. They are civilizing
agencies and routines from which Jews need to gain a certain amount of
detachment, for like all such schedules of existence, they are in constant
need of reformation and reconstruction.[21]

This may, at first sight, sound iconoclastic and disrespecful toward the
traditions of Jewish experience. As explained by Kaplan, however, it shows
a high regard for the past and its heritage, being iconoclastic only in the most
profound sense of prophetic impatience with idols which detract from the
worship of the true God. In describing the characteristics proper to Jewish
ethics, Kaplan extolls the prophetic model of reconstruction, notes that

---

* Baeck, *This People Israel*, p. 23.

ethical principles can and should resort to the past to determine whether or not they are truly aligned with the basic tendencies of human nature, and highly commends the tradition of *torah*-study as a method of community discussion to determine what is right in problems of human conduct.[22]

These emphases lead Kaplan to the conclusion that Judaism's uniqueness lies in a conception of God which emphasizes the control of power more than power itself. He sees his tradition as one which underscores the regulation of the power which humans possess in order to develop peoples' potential for the good life, and for social freedom, justice, and peace. Hence, he argues, there can be no social justice unless the individual realizes his accountability in the responsible use of power, a characteristic emphasis of Judaism understood in reconstructionist terms.[23]

As a culmination to this understanding of Jewish ethics, Kaplan has arrived at six general guidelines which might well be considered mandates for the contemporary Jew. These principles point to the following responsibilities for Jews today:

1. to reaffirm the peoplehood conception of Judaism
2. to revitalize the practice of the Jewish religion
3. to form a network of organic Jewish communities
4. to strengthen the political state of Israel
5. to promote cultural creativity among Jews
6. to cooperate with all men in the pursuit of freedom, justice and peace.[24]

BUBER, HESCHEL, AND SOLOVEITCHIK

Neither Buber nor Heschel have been inclined to spend much time elaborating moral principles. Both have been primarily concerned with the attitudes and assumptions behind them. Buber acknowledges that principles are indeed products of man, but insists that they must be developed out of dialogue with God or will inevitably degenerate into shabby, impersonal, and demeaning regulators of human behavior. Heschel manifests the same concern, and, even in his highly pertinent comments on current moral problems, tends to reduce most of them to "more basic" questions. According to Eugene Borowitz this reductionism not only irritates Heschel's audiences, but also effectively eliminates him from having anything truly concrete and communicable to say about behavior.[25]

While neither Buber nor Heschel spend much time formulating moral principles, it is nevertheless true that the general recommendations they make are indeed functions of their views of man and the theater of life's process. This has been more fully substantiated in earlier chapters, and hence will merely be stated here.

We can, however, get additional insights into the way Buber and Heschel handle moral principles if we recall that they both use the nonlegal rabbinic materials as their principal resources for detailing Jewish ethics. Emphasizing the proclamation, or *haggadic* materials, and sometimes the philosophies of medievalists, mystics and the *hasidim*, they come to a discussion of principles with a somewhat unconventional Jewish point of view.

Joseph B. Soloveitchik provides a striking contrast, more conventionally legal in orientation, and much more concerned with evolving truly concrete and communicable statements about proper behavior. He is thoroughly convinced that it was God who gave man the *Torah* and commanded him to search out its meaning. Therefore, principles, their detailed exegesis and application, are much more important to Soloveitchik. And because they are important we find him interpreting the meaning of man as *ish hahalachah* (halakhic man, the man of the instruction).[26]

Post-reformation Christian ethics. Earlier in this chapter we considered the kinds of statements that arise on the "moral level of discourse" and noted that this chapter would be primarily concerned with statements of moral principles arising on that level of discourse. As we initiate a discussion of moral principles in Christian ethics, a further refinement is in order. This is due to the fact that the principles stated on the moral level by Christian thinkers are quite different than those enunciated by others. As the debates of recent decades have demonstrated, Christian moral thinkers have at least three different convictions about which kinds of principles ought to be offered as norms for behavior.

For these reasons it may be helpful to list and explain these different positions from the start, before treating the role that principles play in each of the four subsystems of Christian ethics as outlined in the paradigms of the last two chapters. For this purpose we shall use a schema proposed by Frederick S. Carney, in which he outlines a *principle(s)* position, a *rules* position, and a *virtue* position, as the three main stances taken by Christian ethicians in the problems associated with moral principles and the role they are to play in decision-making.[27]

1. The first position claims the existence and applicability of some ultimate *principle(s)* in deciding what is to be done. The value of such a principle (or set of principles) for those who hold this position is that it is highly general, indicating simply a quality that must be present in every moral act, and successfully avoiding the hazards of an overburdened or legalistic set of prescriptive principles. In Christian ethics, this position is represented by those who emphasize the primacy and sole necessity of the principle of love. They claim that this norm is sufficient for the Christian, supporting the claim with various interpretations of biblical texts and theological traditions, and resolve that the only norm the Christian need apply is "do the loving thing." Included in this school of thought would be contemporaries such as J. A. T. Robinson and Joseph Fletcher.[28]

2. The second position is one which emphasizes the importance of very detailed and specific directions, normally called *rules* in current discussions of moral principles. It stresses the fact that some rules are absolute or generally valid extensions of the ultimate principle of love, and notes that decisions made without such objective standards are merely intuitional. Among

supporters of this position we would find most traditional Catholic moralists and the Protestant ethician Paul Ramsey.[29]

3. The third position might be called the *virtue* or *context* position, depending on the thinkers to whom the tag is applied. Some emphasize the quality (or virtue) of the person deciding, lay great stress on the criteria of good character formation, and put the decisive focus on a person's disposition to make correct decisions. Some others, with a similar conviction about the importance of virtue, speak more extensively about the context or situation of decision, share the anti-legalistic (or anti-rule) bias of the first position, and like to call themselves situationists or contextualists. Despite this fact, it seems that most of these thinkers have the basic attitudes and orientations of the moral agent as their primary concern, and should, therefore, be more properly called supporters of the position stressing *virtue*. Among thinkers in this group we can include Joseph Sittler.[30]

The above clarification of three different positions on moral principles should better prepare us for the following discussion of the principles factor in four distinct subsystems of Christian ethics. It should aid us in understanding how one system may say "principles" and mean "rules" while yet another may mean "inner dispositions", and still another may want it to signify "an ultimate principle(s)."

THOSE WHO PREFER THE SYMBOLS OF CREATION-FALL-REDEMPTION

As explained earlier, theologians in this general system take the creation-fall-redemption symbols as their main clues to the meaning of world process. In slightly different ways they all emphasize man's dependence (created, fallen, and in need of redemption). These two factors cohere very tightly with their general convictions that, whatever kinds of principles are used, primacy must be given to the "command of God" and to general dispositions of obedience and reverence in the face of what God does in and for man.

With this in mind, we can consider two theologians who support this general system. Both would subscribe to the above digest of their positions, yet both would have differences of opinion about the meaning and function of principles in decision-making. In short, each will side with one or another of the three positions (principle[s], rules, and virtue) and still retain a systematic coherence with the general and common positions on the meaning of man and the processes of the universe.

The first to be considered is Karl Barth, one of Christianity's giants in twentieth-century theology. Barth's early interests had been predominantly those of "crisis theology"—a theology of judgment, namely God's sovereign word and grace confronting man in the troublesome days of the first four decades of our century in Europe.[31] His emphasis was that of the creation-redemption tradition, stressing God's sovereignty and man's dependency, calling man to "hear God," and to be critical of all human constructs of value, purpose and obligation. Consequently, he has always been severely critical of the anthropocentric ethics of the more optimistic theologians of the nineteenth century.[32] For Barth, "man is *not* good . . . a rebel, a sluggard, a hypocrite . . . But there is still more: he is the being whom God has loved, and loves and will love . . ."*

Barth's preference is, therefore, for a theocentric ethic, focusing on the biblical themes of election-creation-reconciliation. What he offers in the way of principles issues forth from this context; his ethics flows from his dogmatics. In his *magnum opus* on *Church Dogmatics* the doctrine of election leads him to talk about the command of God as a claim rooted in election.[33] In Volume III creation is his theme, and matters such as war, suicide, love of neighbor, and vocation are treated in this context.[34] This is where he takes up task of "special ethics,"[35] whereas until this point he had spoken primarily of "general ethics."[36] In general ethics he details general principles such as the general requirement of obedience and the obligation of a Christian to consider God's command as decisive and judging.[37] Special ethics works out of a doctrine of a God who actualizes and preserves the created universe, and the principles he develops pivot around "four freedoms."[38] "*Freedom before God*" requires worship, prayer, and confession (inner and outer witness of faith).[39] "*Freedom in fellowship*" requires honor to our fellow men: in marriage, parent-child relations, and with both close and distant neighbors.[40] "*Freedom for life*" demands respect for one's own life and for the protection of all human life.[41] "*Freedom in limitation*" asks recognition of man's finitude, and spells out special responsibilities accompanying limitation. Man must realize the limited opportunity of his life span, his special call to live well each moment and to shape his tasks responsibly at various stages in his lifetime.[42]

Obviously Barth is not opposed to spelling out both general and specific principles. What he calls "practical casuistry" is quite amenable to his theological convictions, but worlds apart from "theoretical casuistry," which he feels is founded upon man's desire to be autonomous and to devise a system of rules independent of the divine word and command, a ruse which effectively eliminates the need for God.[43] Barth's theocentric ethical principles are sharply contrasted with such anthropocentric norms. His are completely cast in terms of faith and certain key doctrines (God, election, creation, reconciliation).

The principles we have so far considered are incomplete without those he planned to detail in conjunction with the doctrine of reconciliation. Illness, old-age, and finally death foreclosed all possibility of knowing the fullness of Barthian ethics. Some glimmerings of what he planned can, however, be had in the portions of Volume IV from which he intended to draw the ethical implications of reconciliation. Volume IV, part 1 emphasizes the

---

* Karl Barth, *The Humanity of God*, (Richmond: John Knox Press, 1960), p. 60.

humbling of Christ and unmasks man's sin as one of pride, which is overcome by the justifying work of Christ. Volume IV, part 2 highlights the
kingly exaltation of Christ, revealing man's sloth, which is transformed by
the sanctifying power of Christ and His Spirit. Volume IV, part 3 focuses
attention on the person of Christ more than His work, and links man's
vocation to the prophetic witness of Christ reconciling all men in fellowship
with God.

From this latter part of the doctrine, Barth draws implications about
man's vocation (to partake in the ministry of reconciliation),[44] and places
the burden of this vocation in a kind of service called witness.[45] His reflections
on witness and discipleship are extremely profound and far outstrip the
common fare in moralistic thinking about discipleship.[46] He was searching for
a way to identify the goal and essential controlling principle of discipleship
in the larger context of salvation history, and recurrently focused his attention
on the meaning of Christian witness.[47] It is truly unfortunate that we cannot
know the more specific principles which he would have drawn out of this
general command to witness, but we know it includes: living in accordance
with the gifts of the Spirit, daily renewing of one's self, saying "yes" gratefully,
acting with obedience and hope, and freely witnessing to the reconciliation
at work in our midst.[48]

Although we can consider Barth in the grouping of Christian ethicians
who prefer the creation-fall-redemption symbols, we can see from what
appears in the fourth massive volume of the *Church Dogmatics* that he also
devotes time to the symbols of justification, sanctification, and discipleship.
However, even Volume IV reinforces the emphases of his earlier work which
depicted man primarily in terms of his inferior-to-superior relationship to
God. The basic concept in reconciliation ethics is still that of God's command,[49] and the fragment of Volume IV, part 4 repeatedly emphasizes
obedience and subordination as the key attitudes of the Christian *ethos*,
while expressing the divine-human relationship in terms of the gift of grace
given and received.[50]

Paul Lehmann, Auburn Professor of Systematic Theology at Union
Theological Seminary in New York, is another Christian ethician who
comes under the general heading of the creation-redemption system. A self-
styled "contextualist" on the issue of the place of principles in decision-
making, Lehmann has developed a way of handling ethics primarily as a
function of the doctrine of redemption.[51] For Lehmann, this redemption is
communitarian, with the *koinonia* being the locus of God's activity as he tries
". . . to make and to keep human life human."* In his understanding of the
sixteenth-century reformation, what occurred there was a displacement of
the older forms of prescriptive and absolute norms, making ethics "descrip-

* Paul Lehmann, *Ethics in a Christian Context*, (New York: Harper & Row, Publishers,
1963), p. 101.

tive," giving it a task of detailing the concreteness of life and helping man interpret it out of the context of a community in which he experiences forgiveness and reconciliation.[52] Thus, his ". . . main concern . . . is with the concrete ethical reality of a transformed human being and a transformed humanity owing to the specific action of God in Jesus Christ. . . ."*

Furthermore, Lehmann tells us that we should not expect a systematic reflection on what's involved in the ethical claim of Christianity to offer rules for behavior. Its task is one of reflective analysis on the implications of Christian faith, not the prescription of norms telling Christians how to behave.[53] Therefore, conscience is neither *autonomous* (self-directed) nor *heteronomous* (other-directed), but *theonomous* (directed by knowledge of what to do acquired in intimate relationship with God and His community).[54] With this notion of the decision-making faculty of conscience, Lehmann links himself to the teaching of the Apostle Paul and confidently stands on a foundation which repudiates both legalism and anarchy at one and the same time.[55]

We can rightly conclude that his position on principles is one that emphasizes *virtue* or character as the principal consideration in the decision-making process. In his description of ethics we can also identify a functional interrelationship between the author's discussion of conscience—as close as he comes to having a set of principles—his convictions about man and the process created by God's activity. In the latter he differs from Barth only as a particular instance differs from the general case. Both theologians develop ethical reflections which fall within the scope of the Christian subsystem emphasizing the creation-redemption symbols of process, the relational dependence of man on God, and the ever-watchful critique of humanly devised principles of conduct.

THOSE EMPHASIZING

THE SYMBOL OF JUSTIFICATION

Historically speaking the justification subsystem of Christian ethics arose in closest proximity to the full flowering of a Christian legalism and casuistry in the times of late medieval and early renaissance Europe.[56] Quite reasonably, then, we would expect it to take a very critical stand on legalistic and self-justifying ethics,[57] stressing the fact that what justifies man is outside him. If he but confesses his sinfulness, lives by faith, and walks free, he will be doing what is required of the Christian according to this school of thought. Ethics of the justification system is generally called an ethics of faith and hope, the ethics of a man who both hopes and walks confidently in freedom— "*simul iustus et peccator.*" It exhibits a high degree of coherence between its factors, and its principles are usually those of the most general type encouraging attitudes but refraining from detailing rules.

---

* Lehmann, *Ethics in a Christian Context,* p. 17.

However, some theologians in this general category carry the principle-making process somewhat further in the conviction that a Christian must say something more concrete and communicable about the troublesome social and political realities confronting us all. They are not, therefore, unwilling to elaborate principles pertinent to the difficult issues of justice and power.

This line of thought has been called "Christian Realism"[58] and centers around the figure of the American theologian Reinhold Niebuhr, who promoted this emphasis in justification ethics during the 1930's and following. Under his leadership generations of Christians sought to relate their religious faith to social and political questions, deriving norms for behavior with the aid of Niebuhr's writings.

His realism was spawned in polemical interplay with the thought of nineteenth-century liberal optimists, who viewed man more nobly than Niebuhr thought allowed by Christian faith. He countered with statements firmly rooted in Augustinian and Reformation anthropology. He attempted to temper optimism about the possibilities of realizing the love ethic in real life by promoting a view of man which emphasizes the depth and difficulty of evil, and by endorsing a balance-of-power conception of justice as applied to the national problems of labor and industry, trade and foreign affairs.[59] As Niebuhr saw it, Christian ethics must say not only that man is free, but also must address itself to specifying that task to which he is freed. He is free to pursue the cause of justice, to influence the conduct of institutions, with both confidence in his God-given freedom and with a simultaneous humility born of an awareness of his condition of sinfulness. He had also decided that by revising the traditional natural law approach to principles he could offer Christians a valuable means for detailing their task in life's concrete situations.[60] What he seemed to object to most of all in traditional natural law approaches to moral principles was their assumption that there is something fixed and static about human nature. Niebuhr posited a self-transcending human freedom which rose above all such patterns of human nature and defied all natural law principles derived from them. For such a free spirit as man, Niebuhr believed love to be the law of life, but believed that more proximate applications (principles) were also required. In this he finds few immutable norms,[61] but recognizes equality, liberty, and the universal prohibition of murder as minimum requirements of justice.[62]

We can reasonably conclude that Niebuhr is at once representative of the justification system's pattern of coherence between the ethical factors, and, at the same time, more accurately called a promoter of the *principle(s)* position in handling moral statements of obligation.

Before concluding our discussion of the justification system in Christian ethics, we ought to mention, however briefly, the ethics of Rudolf Bultmann. In this theologian we find a style and message that has shaped much of twentieth-century discussion in Christian theology.[63] In his ethical discussion we find abundant evidence of the proclivity to dialectic so common among those who prefer the justification symbol as the hallmark of their understanding of world process. Bultmann's conviction about man is the prevalent one of this group, namely, that people are both sinful and just, "old" and "new." In tight coherence with these first two factors, the principles Bultmann prefers are the paradoxical statements about value, trying to elucidate the tensions between "indicative and imperative, freedom and obedience, gospel and law, radical love and radical obedience."[64] In fact, he seems to prefer not to go much beyond this type of description of the paradoxical nature of the Christian life. His ethical emphasis is on the nature of authentic existence and living up to the demands of the existential moment. Beyond that he says little, and seems to feel that man simply knows what is good and needs no further specifications in the way of principles. Hence he gives none.[65]

In light of the above Bultmann can be considered in the general category of justification ethics (paradox in process, people, and principles), as one who takes his stand on principles in a way similar to those who emphasize the importance of *virtue* or *character formation* in decision making.

THOSE WHO PREFER

THE SANCTIFICATION SYMBOL

John Wesley had much in common with several different strains of Christian ethics, such as the pietism of the Reformers, the devotion-discipline emphases of high-church Anglicans, and the manuals of spiritual discipline from Roman Catholic sources.[66] With an over-riding emphasis on striving for perfection, Wesley continually stressed the imitation of Christ and the following of the law of love as steps along this road.[67] Furthermore, he outlined several dangers for man, who is at once both sinful and saved, noting how failures to pray enough, giving into evil thoughts and tempers, losing faith or becoming weak in witness would cause a man to fall from grace.[68]

In his preaching Wesley was spelling out a set of both positive and negative principles for behavior. However, he resolutely refused to focus on the details and consequences of conduct, stressing the fact that motives and purposes are the most important considerations. This is entirely coherent with his understanding of process and people as detailed earlier. Wesley's principles, general as they are, are clearly consistent with his understanding of man who is in the precarious position of being filled with grace and yet ever in danger of reverting to sin. The process is what God does through the Spirit, transforming will, intention, and motive. What we need, therefore, are suggestions as to how we might cooperate in this process and remain on the path to perfection. This, Wesley supplies in the form of very general guidelines of disciplined piety and rigorous practices of self-giving love. Such recommendations as he gives are, therefore, in the category of the *principle(s)* position which values moral principles that simply indicate a quality that ought to be present in every moral act.

If Wesley's system seems simple enough, the same cannot be said of the other tradition normally considered under the title of sanctification ethics, namely that of the Roman Catholic schools of moral theology, focused from time to time around the figure of Thomas Aquinas. These schools show a high degree of diversity depending on their allegiance to Alphonsus Liguori, Suarez, or Aquinas. Since the nineteenth century, however, they have all attempted to demonstrate their consistency with the methods and principles of Aquinas.[69] The Catholic tradition in moral theology is best known for its procedures in natural law and casuistry, rooted in Suarezian and Liguorian sources, with some minor reliance on Aquinas. More recent developments, however, have focused on Thomas with greater skill and interest, making it quite difficult to indulge in easy caricatures of Catholic theology as legalistic and naturalistic.

Therefore, in dealing with the principles factor in Catholic systems of ethics, we shall have to take two directions. First of all, we shall demonstrate the consistency of traditional casuistic and legalistic principles with its accompanying view of process and people. Secondly, we shall emphasize the coherence of Thomistic principles with the other two factors in Aquinas' system.

There has been a long-standing Catholic tradition of casuistry (solving moral dilemmas by the use of paradigm cases) and legalism (elaborate systems of detailed rules for behavior, constructed, administered, and interpreted by lawfully appointed authorities -moral theologians, canonists, and varying grades of ordained administrators with "jurisdiction" over the believers of the community). The general process view underpinning this approach is one that sees men as travellers on their way to an eternal goal. People are naturally good but weakened, if not impotent, when it comes to reaching a goal far beyond the natural powers of man. Therefore, they stand in need of revealed directives for this journey, and require clear and forceful prodding to be led along the path. Furthermore, they tend to falter and need to be stirred on by strong sanctions built into the law. Therefore, while all laws are not of equal importance, they are all helpful and to be taken seriously.

The principles factor in this system is quite coherent with its accompanying views of man and world process. As a position on principles it emphasizes rules more than ultimate principles or virtuous character. However, it not only stresses some rules as absolute or generally valid, but emphasizes the importance of all rules. This naturally tends to blur the distinctions between laws (human or divine, moral or ecclesiastical) and the nuances of difference are almost exclusively the domain of learned experts who have taken the time to learn the origin and justification behind particular laws. Consequently, the common man following this system conscientiously becomes more and more dependent on the judgments of others to help him decide what he ought to do, and, as some argue, actually loses what the virtue position emphasizes—character!

When legalistic ethics is berated, it is usually this managing of detailed principles which is being criticized. Both Nietzsche and Fromm have underscored its weakness, calling it either a "slave ethic" or a dehumanizing "authoritarian ethic." Catholics themselves have seen its weaknesses and ill effects, bringing to the fore equally traditional systems of ethics during the recent decades of feverish renewal in moral theology.[70]

The principal alternative offered since the late nineteenth century is that of the Thomistic tradition, the second variety of Catholic views on principles which can be considered under the general heading of the sanctification system. The last chapter drew attention to the importance of the Thomist scheme of virtues (theological, intellectual, moral, and the gifts of the Spirit).[71] The set of principles elaborated by Aquinas is a direct function of the same scheme. Correlative to the theological virtues are principles for behavior indicating what ought to be done in order to remain faithful, hopeful, and full of charity.[72] Correlative to prudence, wisdom, knowledge, and other intellectual virtues we find a set of rules pointing out behavior suited to sustaining these God-given habits. The same is true in the case of the moral virtues of justice, fortitude and temperance, which also require guidelines indicating the inner and outer limits of behavior considered suited to these virtues. All these different principles can be considered as nothing more than logical consequences of the meaning of a person transformed by the power of Christ's Spirit. The "new law" working in the hearts of men is recast in the form of the particularized powers of man (using the Aristotelian analogy of the soul and its faculties), and is conjugated into directives for behavior befitting a man so affected by grace. The Thomistic position is, therefore, a consistent interplay of process, people, and principles factors, as well as a rules-type position on the use of moral guidelines.

Yet, Aquinas had more to say about laws and rules, sometimes using analogies built on the movement of God creating, providing for, and governing the natural universe, sometimes building on medieval analogies of authority, law and society, and sometimes building on the analogy of man seeking perfect happiness and fulfillment in his final destiny.[73] Thus, he is read differently by different interpreters. But the prevalent direction of Thomistic moral studies emphasizes the virtues scheme since, as it is alleged, it is "more Christian," and as I believe, a surer route to reinterpreting a moral theology overburdened with legalities.

Whatever nuances of interpretation may be given the Wesleyan and Thomistic traditions, they both seem to be constituted by coherence between their views of life as a process of sanctification, man as the subject of this transforming power, and principles structured to aid and abet the continued perfecting of what was begun by grace.

The general advice given by Christian ethicians in this system is to follow or imitate Christ. However, this general counsel is translated into several strains of meaning, some very subtle and others more crassly literal.

In the more subtle varieties we find semi-mystical endorsements of being like Christ, suggesting that Christians must be "conformed" to Him in obedience, suffering, and lowliness. Thus, Soren Kierkegaard details the requirements of being Christ-like in a portrait of demanding self-humiliation and suffering, self-denial and social rejection.[74] Similarly, Dietrich Bonhoeffer calls for patterning one's life on the obedient, lowly, and humble Christ, demanding asceticism and discipline, avoiding "cheap grace" in a "costly discipleship."[75] For these and others,[76] Christ is the pattern, the expression of true righteousness, and by conforming themselves to Him Christians similarly become living signs of godliness, active testimonies to the workings of God within man.

This line of thought can be termed semi-mystical for several reasons. It is, first of all, quite consciously in opposition to the rationalistic emphasis of ethical optimists who set Christ up as an "ideal man," a heroic image of man's self-fulfillment. In countering this emphasis which permeated their ethical environment, Kierkegaard and Bonhoeffer tried to demonstrate the paradox of the Christian life in which a man is fulfilled by losing himself. Secondly, this group plays down the value of principles and rules as misleading guides, and favors instead the emphasis on the fully flexible kind of behavior proper to one who is transformed in a virtuous relationship with God through Christ. Finally, it utilizes a set of principles which are rooted in the Pauline and Johannine theologies of the process as a mystical relationship of people to Christ.[77] It is well represented in a statement such as the following from Bernard Häring:

> It is possible for us to follow Christ, to imitate Him, because He is the "Word" in whom our likeness to God rests and through whom it has been wonderfully restored by the Redemption. In the fulfillment of the imitation, our likeness to God becomes manifest. And just as all discussion about an image refers back to the original or prototype which has been copied, so too must moral theology direct the Christian life in all points to the Word or Logos, the divine pattern in whom and through whom man made to the divine image lives and to whom he can respond.*

* Bernard Häring, *The Law of Christ*, Vol. I (Westminster: Newman, 1961), pp. 52–53.

We have included in the discipleship system theologians whose understanding of man and world process is quite different from, and in fact, polemically opposed to the views of most nineteenth-century theologians. Yet, the principles suggested by these theologians are discipleship principles and can well be considered here if only by reason of the counterposition they take in reference to more optimistic views of man and the process.

There are still others in the category of discipleship ethics whose emphasis is not so much on Christ as a pattern, and who prefer to give their attention to the teachings of Jesus.[78] In this latter group there are also several shades of difference in the interpretations given the teachings of Jesus. Some[79] see in these teachings the mandate of a certain attitude toward life; others find that they contain a basic direction, pointing out a general way through life without giving authoritative or always applicable rules; still others see in Jesus a new law, a new norm for life, focusing primarily on the uniqueness and simplicity of his command.[80]

Most of these differences of opinion begin with and center on the Sermon on the Mount. All agree that the precepts given there are to be taken seriously, but then proceed to differ widely on just what is implied in taking them seriously. Biblical scholarship (especially historical and form criticism) has raised a host of problems that add to the difficulties for proponents of this view, calling into question the very nature of the document with which they begin their studies. Hence differences in opinion about the commandment(s) given by Jesus can be traced back to differences in opinion on the nature and extent of the revealed character of the New Testament. Uncertainty about the authorization behind the Sermon's statements has led many to emphasize the "essentials" as attitudes or directions. Yet some are not at all uncertain on this matter and consider the whole of the Sermon a fully authorized divine revelation. Such biblical fundamentalism is operative in what Carl F. H. Henry has to say about the will of God particularized in the Sermon, which, for him, is a set of norms to be followed literally.[81] Since the Bible is primarily a book of divinely revealed morality for Henry, its prescriptions are authoritative and demand literal obedience of the believer.

This certainly represents a *rules* position on the function of principles in Christian ethics. It not only accepts the authenticity of God's will as expressed in the biblical words, but enjoins a literal obedience upon those who would call themselves followers of Christ.

The Muslim religious ethic. When the Muslim sets out on a life of submission to Allah, he has a set of principles which provide a sure footing along all the landmarks of his path. As he embarks on a life of actualizing the will of his God, he gives primacy to a principle found repeatedly in the Qu'ran, that is, the saved, happy, or successful man is the one "who believed and did the good."[82] Islam is unanimously defined by Muslims as "conviction and action,"[83] thereby underlining their overarching guideline for human behavior.

In addition to this all-encompassing norm, Muslims accept the principles commonly called the "Five Pillars," as contained in the Qu'ran.[84] In these five categories the Muslim finds further specification of the imperative to believe and do the good. The Pillars upon which Islam is founded command:

1. The confession of and witness to Allah
2. Prayer
3. Sharing of Wealth (Almsgiving)
4. Fasting (such as the Ramadan)
5. Pilgrimage (to Mecca)

In addition to this minimum Muslim observance, there are countless numbers of principles contained in the Qu'ran which are, however, synthesized in a variety of intellectual systems. As in the two preceding chapters, we shall consider just one of these systems, namely, the one put forward by M. Moinuddin Siddiqui in the *Islamic Correspondence Course*.[85] He ties the bulk of the Qu'ran's ethical principles together under the concept of a truly balanced life, which, he notes, is the ideal of the Islamic moral teaching.[86] A truly balanced life is one that achieves equilibrium by keeping the five pillars in proper perspective, and not allowing one or another to become an all-encompassing obsession. In addition to this sense of balance, the Muslim should also find the proper proportions for the following obligations: building personal character, concern for interpersonal relationships, responsibility in social ties (family, neighbors, and the needy), and zeal in economic and administrative affairs.[87]

While synthesizing these various dimensions of Muslim obligation under the specific heading of "a balanced life," Siddiqui is, nevertheless, giving a faithful rendering of the principles of the Qu'ran, principles which all Muslim thinkers accept as normative, even if they sometimes prefer organizing concepts different than the one we are considering here. Siddiqui's conclusion gives another most general principle of Muslim morality, and one to which all Muslim thinkers give abundant commentary, namely, the principle of *Jihad* ("striving"—in the cause of God). *Jihad* is presented as the motivating principle of Muslim zeal for all areas of human life. It links ethical norms with the Muslim conviction about people (who are basically good, constituted in a basic unity by God), as well as their interpretation of life's process as an earnest pursuit of the goal of felicity. Striving in the cause of God is seen by Siddiqui and others as a summary of the Muslim ethic, which moves men to intellectual activities like education and persuasive argumentation, as well as to social involvement in all causes affecting human welfare.[88]

As we conclude this sampling of ethical principles coming from several different traditions of religious ethics, we may be better able to understand a comment made by a man who has observed religious ethics from the vantage point of one interested in signs, values, and human behavior: "Thus the religions, in prescribing how one should act, rest their case upon appraisals as to what is good, and these in turn are made in the light of statements as to the nature of man and the world."*

STUDY QUESTIONS

1. How influential are religious moral principles in your home, town, city today?

2. Would the Taoist set of ethical principles be more suitable than those from Judaism and Christianity in our attempts to relate sensibly with our natural environment?

3. Is it true to say that all Buddhist moral principles are highly individualistic and concerned with personal salvation only?

4. Consider Abraham Heschel's comments about war in the 1960's. Are his principles coherent with his stated views about process and people? Are they sufficiently concrete to be useful in governmental decisions?

5. Under which symbol would you classify the Christian ethics of Helmut Thielicke? Jacque Ellul? Billy Graham?

6. Do Christian ministers who are primarily concerned with pastoral ministry generally tend to prefer the discipleship symbols? Are they less concerned than others about the theological underpinnings of ethical statements?

7. Consider the moderate stance of John Bennett during the "new morality debate." Identify the factors in his "system," and determine their coherence on the basis of the "good story" criterion.

8. Is natural law thinking on the increase in ethical considerations? Should it be? Would it promote mutual understanding and agreement on world problems more readily than specifically religious moral principles?

NOTES

1. Note that some theologians prefer to use the word "principles" only when referring to very general suggestions like "love your neighbor" or "be prudent," and use the term "rules" for particularized statements like "you must pay five per cent sales tax on all commodities" or "a Christian cannot participate in a nuclear war." Cf. Paul Ramsey, "The Case of the Curious Exception" and James Gustafson, "Moral Discernment in the Christian Life," in *Norm and Context in Christian Ethics,* Gene Outka, Paul Ramsey, eds. (New York: Charles Scribner's Sons, 1968), p. 67 ff. and p. 17 ff. respectively.

2. After suggesting the utility of Aiken's model for our present study, we should note two qualifications that may help avert some misunderstandings. First of all,

* William Morris, *Signification and Significance,* (Cambridge: The M.I.T. Press, 1964), p. 37.

many will want to remind me that the ordinary "garden-variety" of principles used in much of human activity are those which originate on the expressive-evocative level. Secondly, the model used here may well be pictured as a circle, with the commitments of the post-ethical level affecting the expressive-evocative and moral levels of discourse. I wish to express my agreement with both qualifications, and confess that this study's emphasis on the moral level of discourse is due to my conviction that the formulators of religious ethics usually make their statements on this level and encourage their hearers to both assent to and operate on the basis of such principles. Therefore, within the limits of this study's objectives we are narrowing our discussion to just one level of moral discourse, without intending to imply that this gives a full account of the complexity of the factors operating in observable human behavior.

3. Noss, *Man's Religions*, p. 282 ff.

4. Lin Yutang, *The Wisdom of Confucius* (New York: Random House, Inc., 1938), p. 13.

5. Cf. *Sources of Chinese Tradition*, Vol. I, pp. 259–65.

6. *The Sayings of Lao-tzu* (Wisdom of the East series), ed. John Murray, (London, 1905), p. 34 (#LXI).

7. Ninian Smart, *The Religious Experience of Mankind*, p. 76 ff.

8. Von Glasenapp, *Non-Christian Religions, A to Z*, p. 34 ff.

9. *ibid.*, (esp. p. 37).

10. Smart, *op. cit.*, pp. 83–84.

11. Von Glasenapp, *op. cit.*, p. 41.

12. Cf. Baeck's articles in Simon Bernfeld's *The Foundations of Jewish Ethics*, A. H. Koller, translator (New York: KTAV Publishing House, Inc., 1968) rev. ed. of original 1929 edition; Cf. also Leo Baeck, *The Essence of Judaism* (New York: Schocken Books, Inc., 1948) [reprint and revision by Irving Howe of the original 1905 edition], p. 60, from which the following quotation is taken: "Nothing like this birth of monotheism out of Israel's moral consciousness has ever occurred elsewhere in history."

13. Baeck, *The Essence of Judaism*, p. 80.

14. *op. cit.*, pp. 87, 90, 150, 152, 155.

15. *op. cit.*, p. 148.

16. *This People Israel*, p. 399; Cf. contrast with footnote 14.

17. *This People Israel*, pp. 74, 75, 401.

18. Cf. Borowitz, *A New Jewish Theology in the Making*, p. 80, and Friedlander's introduction to *This People Israel*, p. x, where he claims that Baeck has, by this time, both reconciled and transcended the thought of both Buber and Rosenzweig.

19. Cf. Mordecai Kaplan, *The Greater Judaism in the Making* (New York: The Reconstructionist Press, 1960).

20. Mordecai Kaplan, *Judaism as a Civilization* (New York: Thomas Yoseloff, Inc., 1957; reprint of original 1934 edition), pp. 432, 433.

21. *op. cit.*, pp. 413–14.

22. *op. cit.*, chapter XXX "Jewish Ethics", pp. 460–78.

23. *The Greater Judaism in the Making*, pp. 482–83.

24. *op. cit.*, pp. 484–87; cf. also the 1957 preface to the 1934 book *Judaism as a Civilization*, p. x.

25. Borowitz, *op. cit.*, pp. 157–58.

26. *op. cit.*, p. 160 ff., cf. also chapter three of this text, pp. 76–77.

27. Cf. "Deciding in the Situation: What is Required?" in *Norm and Context in Christian Ethics*, p. 3 ff.

28. Cf. Robinson's *Honest to God* (London: SCM, 1963), and *Christian Morals Today* (Philadelphia: Westminster, 1964); Cf. also Eletcher's *Situation Ethics* (Philadelphia: The Westminster Press, 1966).

29. Cf. his *Deeds and Rules in Christian Ethics* (New York: Charles Scribner's Sons, 1967), as well as Roman Catholic manuals of moral theology, including the highly creative and contemporary Bernard Haring's *The Law of Christ*.

30. Cf. his *The Structure of Christian Ethics* (Baton Rouge, 1958).

31. From the late 1930's to the late 1940's, however, Barth's emphasis shifted to focus more intently on the message of God's grace (vs. His law, wrath, accusation, and judgment), without, however, suppressing his concern to talk about the latter continuously.

32. Cf. *Revolutionary Theology in the Making: Barth-Thurneysen Correspondence*, trans. James D. Smart (Richmond: John Knox Press, 1964).

33. *Church Dogmatics*, II: 2.

34. *Church Dogmatics*, III: 4 (Edinburgh: T. & T. Clark, 1961).

35. *op. cit.*, p. 3.

36. *Church Dogmatics*, II: 2, #36.

37. *op. cit.*, #'s 37–39.

38. *Church Dogmatics*, III: 4, #'s 53–56. Note: the full form of Barthian ethics awaited the completion of IV/4, "The Command of God the Reconciler", and remained unpublished at the time of his death, except for IV/4, fragment, mentioned below (fn. 50).

39. *Church Dogmatics*, III: 4, #53, p. 47 ff.

40. *op. cit.*, #54, p. 116 ff.

41. *op.* #55, p. 324 ff.

42. *op. cit.*, #56, p. 565 ff.

43. *op. cit.*, pp. 6–18.

44. Karl Barth, *Church Dogmatics*, Vol. IV, Part 3, Second Half (IV: 3: II), Bromiley and Torrance, eds. (Edinburgh: T. & T. Clark, 1962), pp. 482–84.

45. *op. cit.*, pp. 603–14.

46. *op. cit.*, pp. 558–59.

47. *op. cit.*, pp. 521–39, 556, 603–14.

48. *op. cit.*, pp. 39, 40, 42, 106.

49. *op. cit.*, p. 610.

50. Karl Barth, *Church Dogmatics*, Vol. IV, Part 4, Fragment, Bromiley and Torrance, eds. (Edinburgh: T. & T. Clark, 1969). pp. 35–36, 41–43.

51. This does not intend to imply that Lehmann's theology focuses exclusively on the redemption theme, but rather that, in contrast to Barth, whose published materials have focused primarily on the creation-election aspects, Lehmann has focused *primarily* on the redemption aspects.

52. *Ethics in a Christian Context*, pp. 15, 17.

53. *op. cit.*, p. 23.

54. *op. cit.*, pp. 347–52.

55. *op. cit.*, pp. 354–60. Note: Lehmann finds this interpretation most incisively and succintly put in Calvin's *Institutes* Book III, Cf. Lehmann's reference to same in *op. cit.*, p. 365.

56. Cf. K. S. Latourette, *A History of Christianity* (New York: Harper & Row, Publishers, 1953).

57. i.e., a kind of ethics which, by emphasizing the importance of living up to an elaborate and detailed set of rules, begins to deceive man into thinking that he is thereby saving himself.

58. Cf. "Christian Realism: A Symposium" in *Christianity and Crisis*. **28** : 14 (August 5, 1968).

59. Cf. R. Niebuhr, *An Interpretation of Christian Ethics*, (New York: Harper & Row, Publishers, 1935), pp. 105, 110; and *The Nature and Destiny of Man*, Vol. II (New York: Charles Scribner's Sons, 1943), Sect. II and III.

60. Cf. his essay "Love and Law in Protestantism and Catholicism" in *Christian Realism and Political Problems* (New York: Charles Scribner's Sons, 1953), c. 10.

61. Cf. his *Faith and History* (New York: Charles Scribner's Sons, 1949), p. 183.

62. Cf. *The Nature and Destiny of Man*, vol. II, p. 254, and *An Interpretation of Christian Ethics*, pp. 149, 150, 196.

63. Cf. his *Theology of the New Testament*, 2 vols., K. Grobel, translator (New York: Charles Scribner's Sons, 1951, 1955); cf. also R. Bultmann and others, *Kerygma and Myth*, H. W. Bartsch, editor (New York: Harper & Row, Publishers, 1961).

64. Thomas Oden, *Radical Obedience* (*The Ethics of Rudolf Bultmann*) (Philadelphia: The Westminster Press, 1964), c. IV.

65. *op. cit.*, p. 122, and Bultmann's response on p. 144. Note: Bultmann is usually considered an "existentialist" in theology, and utilizes the thought and categories of Martin Heidegger.

66. Gustafson, *Christ and the Moral Life*, p. 83.

67. Cf. his *Sermons*, vol. II, p. 286.

68. *Sermons*, vol. I, p. 307.

69. This comment does not intend to ignore the revival of interest in Aquinas which occurred in the seventeenth century. Rather, it emphasizes the author's conviction that this particular revival, limited almost exclusively to "commentaries" on the works of Aquinas, was less important than the one begun in the nineteenth century, utilizing "modern" methods of historical and critical scholarship of the original sources and texts of Aquinas. Furthermore, it was the nineteenth century Thomistic revival which led to the writing of disciplinary canons governing scholar-

ship in the Code of Canon Law, and the disciplinary statements in the 1932 encyclical of Pope Pius XI, entitled "Deus Scientiarum Dominus".

70. Cf. Gerard Gilleman, *The Primacy of Charity in Moral Theology*, and Bernard Haring, *The Law of Christ*.

71. Cf. Chapter III of this text, pp. 82–83.

72. Cf. Gilleman, *op. cit.*

73. Cf. his *Summa Theologiae*, I-II, q. 90 ff.

74. Cf. his *Training in Christianity* (Princeton: Princeton University Press, 1941), pp. 173–232.

75. Cf. his *The Cost of Discipleship* (New York: The Macmillan Company, 1963); Cf. also the theme of "being forsaken" and its place in Bonhoeffer's theology as treated by John Godsey, *The Theology of Dietrich Bonhoeffer* (Philadelphia: The Westminster Press, 1960).

76. Joseph Sittler, *The Structure of Christian Ethics*.

77. Cf. also the "image theology" of Early Church Fathers like Origen, Irenaeus, and Clement of Alexandria.

78. Cf. Gustafson's *Christ and The Moral Life*, cc. V, VI.

79. including Bultmann.

80. Cf. Lutheran studies on the "uses" of the law, Catholic studies in Thomistic understandings of "divine" law, Haring's work, and the work of Joseph Fletcher.

81. Cf. his *Christian Personal Ethics* (Grand Rapids, 1957), pp. 146, 193, and especially p. 325 where he refers to the Sermon on the Mount as an "ethical directory".

82. Isma'il Rāgī al Fārūqī, "Islam", in *The Great Asian Religions*, p. 313.

83. *op. cit., loc. cit.*, p. 312.

84. *The Great Asian Religions*, pp. 348–49; Cf. also M. Moinuddin Siddiqui, *Islamic Correspondence Course*, Units 3, 4, 5a, 5h.

85. Siddiqui, *op. cit.*, Unit 8.

86. *op. cit.*, p. 3.

87. *op. cit.*, pp. 6–16.

88. *op. cit.*, pp. 15–16; Cf. also *The Great Asian Religions*, pp. 349–50.

chapter five

Prospects

WE MIGHT WELL BEGIN THIS CHAPTER with a question asking: What can be learned from our consideration of the art of religious ethics? After many pages discussing three main factors in several varieties of religious ethics, you might well wonder what values or practical skills can be realized and made useful in our turbulent age. The method of our study has thus far been one in which we have considered various religious traditions from the viewpoint of the detached-within,[1] one which does not seek a commitment to any particular ethic in preference to others. You might, therefore, wonder just what the author considers to be of value in such a study, and are entitled to as clear an answer as I can produce.

Throughout this study we have concentrated on what we are calling "the art of religious ethics," which, it seems to me, is less a religious art than it is a human art practiced by religious artists and thinkers. The arts of symbolizing, thinking about, planning and proceeding are clearly common to all men, but so too is the art of keeping process, people, and principles in functional coherence in any attempt to sketch out the meaning and direction of human behavior. In this chapter we shall consider the possibility of applying this latter art to matters of pressing social and political concern in the United States. We might provisionally describe it as something of a "grid" which we can superimpose on problems of behavior in order to see the factors and interrelationships a bit more clearly.

Lest you be tempted to consider this suggestion as just one more technique in an already overwhelmingly technological world, let me say what I believe to be true about the resources we humans have and how they should be developed. First of all, I believe that we have undreamed-of potential as human beings, but that most of our educational preparation draws on a very restricted portion of this potential, channelling it into extremely narrow conduits which lead to specific jobs. In an age such as ours, characterized as it is by rapid change and mounting dangers of future-shock* many believe that specific job-training will become less and less desirable. It is becoming increasingly difficult to prepare anyone with solutions for any precise set of future conditions, and so, as Robert M. Hutchins notes in speaking of the student of today: ". . . if we try to get him ready for something, it may not be there when we have got him ready."†

As Hutchins observes, the technical skills acquired today have an obsolescence rate directly proportionate to the problems they aim at controlling, and the effort of education ought rather to be one of putting the student in "complete possession of all his powers."² Stated in these general terms, we are but restating the traditional ideal of humanistic education, namely, a training in being human, which leads out ("e-ducation") and frees the potential in a man.

There are, however, many different ways of possessing one's own powers and becoming the conscious and deliberative steersmen of our behavior. We must, therefore, be more specific about the particular way we are suggesting in this study. To be specific I must point out a second conviction, namely, that one who is to possess his own powers must develop one of a variety of what may be called "survival strategies." If one is to survive the intellectual and social pressures of life in community with others, and to maintain a modicum of self-possession and openness to developing his potential, he must develop some techniques which prohibit his being captivated by the images of reality held by the community in which he happened to be born. Some of the best educators in history have been people who tried to help their contemporaries see that even the most cherished beliefs of society were frequently misconceptions, faulty assumptions, superstitions, and boldfaced lies. This may, at first sight, sound iconoclastic and opposed to commitments of any kind, but, in fact, is simply a way of reminding ourselves that icons should have a limited term of office and that irrevocable commitments are often so visceral as to close off rationality and any new visions of life.

When people discover that the world they were trained to believe in does not really exist, and that its images of reality are mirages which disappear on contact, they may capitulate to irrationality as a way of life, become rebellious and sacriligeous iconclasts, or withdraw completely from the political, social, and religious activities of men. Since none of these appear

---

* Disorientation in one's environment due to accelerated rate of change in society.

† Reprinted, by permission, from the September, 1968 issue of *The Center Magazine*, a publication of the Center for the Study of Democratic Institutions in Santa Barbara, California, p. 3.

to be truly fulfilling alternatives, what I suggest here is a "survival technique" which does not flee from contradictions, capitulate to irrationality, or try to escape provisional but essential commitments. Working on the conviction that the distortions of reality can be identified and exposed, their failure to reach announced goals recognized and remedied, we can consider a method of critically assessing and reconstructing the stories which underpin the behavior of individuals and communities.

With the plethora of information about social and political systems available to us today, we are often discouraged by the immensity of the problem of changing even the tiniest portion of our social environment. The macro-systems that are our social and political institutions imply the *control* of behavior and quickly bring to the fore considerations of power, adminis-tration, input-output energies, and feedback from the people under their sway. In the face of this reality our simple systems analogy pales and appears extremely inadequate to help us understand and stand free in the face of such complex systems. We really require a more complex analogy of a con-trol system, showing nuances in types of control systems (on-off, propor-tional), and dealing with public feedback, its routes and roadblocks.[3] When we were dealing with the various systems of religious ethics, however, we made a studious effort to prescind from a discussion of the socio-political uses to which they have been fitted throughout the course of history. We did this for several reasons, among which was the conviction that it is all too easy to turn discussions of religious ethics into treatises of social or political science and fail to attend to the underlying stories which justify them, and to which large numbers of men give credence. In like manner, it is much too easy to treat social and political questions solely in terms of power struc-tures and tactics of change without ever attending to the stories which launched and maintain the motivating appeal of these institutions. For example, we could hardly imagine an intelligent discussion of marriage and divorce proceedings without some mention of the coherent story of the value of monogamous marriage which animates this aspect of American society.

With these reasons in mind, what we suggest in this chapter is an extension of the human art noticed in the functioning of religious ethics. If it is, as I believe, helpful in understanding the interrelationships of the factors in religious moral teaching, it may also be helpful in getting some leverage in social and political stories. If I am correct in this, then we will have a method of approach that is a once both freeing and fruitful. It can possibly provide sufficient objective distance from the personal and societal beliefs which tend to diminish one's hold on his own powers, and yet give a productive beginning in the critical reconstruction of very large social systems built around one or more justifying symbols, plans or schemes.

The Art of Criticism

There has been no lack of criticism from nearly every quarter in recent years. A host of salvos has been directed at all areas of institutionalized government and society, ranging from penetrating critiques of their basic assumptions and tactics to revolutionary styles of cynicism, disruption and confrontation. Given this situation, it is imperative that we come to some agreement on precisely what kind of criticism we have in mind in this study, and appeal to the root meaning of the Greek word *krisis* ("judgment") as our foundation. To judge means to identify elements in a situation, plan or procedure, to grasp their relationships, and to decide whether or not they are coherent. The standard of coherence used as the norm is that of the harmonious relationship of parts. It is the application of two rules inferred from our study of religious ethics: (1) that systems of religious ethics arise and change by coordinating their process, people, and principles factors; (2) that a functional dissonance between these factors is one of the main causes for reorganization and change.

These criteria of coherence can be applied to an example such as the case of a welfare practice which has a noble interpretation of the worth of a human being, and a set of principles (procedural rules) which destroy the self-estimate of welfare recipients. In suggesting this particular example we only intend to point out that many social and political systems should be criticized, or judged, not so much on the grounds that they fail to implement their noble goals, but rather on the basis of a conviction that this failure is due to inconsistency between the various key factors in the system itself. As in our example, some rule of procedure may well be inconsistent with the system's view of man (and possibly with its notion of the social process as well), thereby creating an inevitable failure to attain its goals. The old truism that "there is nothing wrong with the system except its personnel" may not be as helpful as commonly thought. Not only is system failure possible, but it may well be due to an inherent inconsistency in the "story" which generates and maintains it. One approach to a critical examination of social and political problems, therefore, is a method of examining and evaluating the coherence of the stories which underpin their day-to-day operations.

While it is a modest goal, it is by no means easily attained, since there are many stories underpinning American life, and they are often mutually contradictory, even in the case of a set of stories held in common by one particular group. This should not upset us unduly, however, since we are a people pluralistic by both tradition and conviction, and should expect a plurality of stories. What concerns us most, however, are those stories which have eminently concrete consequences in public affairs. While Americans may hold widely divergent views on the purpose of foreign affairs, the secretary of state and his offices will be working out their daily problems on the basis of some particular administration's understanding of our national aims and goals. To take another example from the realm of interpersonal relations, we might say that we surely expect every couple to make their own story of life together, but we are all, nevertheless, affected by the "official story" implied in civil laws concerning marriage and divorce.

The art of criticism, therefore, is a skill involving the identification and evaluation of these stories. We judge them by sorting out the factors involved and evaluating the degree of consistency between them. Skills such as this are acquired only by practice, and so I suggest the following areas of American life as possible targets for your criticism.[4]

DOMESTIC ISSUES[5]

Under this heading we can include a wide variety of issues embracing the areas of racial, economic, educational, and criminal problems facing the country today. This study suggests that all the public policies developed over the years are principles functionally related to certain notions of people and the process of our lives.

One excellent example of the importance of having a coherent story can be seen in the matter of public education and its relationship to the national welfare. The example can be framed in terms of the traditional tension between "liberal (or general) education" and "technical (or specialized) education." The latter represents a view of education as a process of maintaining our national health and power by training people to become skillful in the crafts required to sustain and enhance this national stance. The instinctive man of action (tough, practical, and hard-headed) is idealized as the kind of person needed, and, therefore, what we ought to become. Accordingly, there are educational principles and legislative guidelines and budgets which both further and support the story of technical and specialized education.

The story of a liberal education is much more difficult to tell convincingly, gets couched in terms that are considered idealistic and too general, and is, therefore, not always persuasive in a pragmatic civilization such as ours. The goal of the process of liberal education is usually stated as that of developing the whole of a man, or aiding him in developing his potential. It emphasizes the dignity, worth, and the potential of men who are to be understood as goals in themselves, and not as servo-mechanisms in the conversion of energy into useful commodities. Its principles, barely marketable in the clearing houses of practical living, endorse such things as truth, beauty, and goodness, learning for the sake of developing a skill in using that particular potential, and the development of tastes and commitments to values in human life.

However, as noted above, this story is neither easily nor often told very well, open as it is to fuzzy generalization, and often used to cloak lack of clarity or precision. Hence, the ideal of this story, the learned or intellectual person, is easily caricatured and demeaned by promoters of the alternative story of education. You can find any number of examples of slurs against the intellectual in the campaign oratory of certain politicians,[6] as well as in the reasoning behind choices of cabinet and advisors for recent Presidents of this country.[7] Many interesting studies could result from a pursuit of these cases. Critical examination of the varying educational policies and programs in different federal administrations during the sixties would supply a curious student with weeks of fascinating research.

Another, and perhaps more pressing human issue, has been that of the race problem in America. Here too we find stories underlying the overt policies and behavior of all institutions in the country. Several views of the *process* have been suggested during the racial conflicts of recent decades. Some have seen the credibility of the American promise and its democratic procedures at stake. Others have viewed it as a test of Christianity, and still others as a process of revolutionary overthrow of the power structures presently impeding true achievement of equal opportunity. The *people* factor in the stories surrounding racial conflict is more interesting still. Within the Negro community itself a high diversity of preferences has developed around identifying images, such as Black, Negro, and Afro-American, and an equally diverse set of values has been attached to slur images such as nigger and Uncle Tom. Within the white community self-identifying appelations like "The Southerner"[8] have proven to be behind many of the rules concocted in the South, while elsewhere whites have been plagued with the "pop" science of stories of racial and cultural inferiority attributed to non-whites. In fact, every coherent story about the racial problem, whether from the black or the white community, has worked on the basis of a dynamic image of self and others which we can, in our terms, call the people factor.

Finally, the behavioral *principles* suggested to solve the racial problem are functions of the person or group's convictions about people and the process in which we are engaged. Revolutionary process views are translated into a coherent story with conflict principles and tactful guidelines. Bi-racial ("separate but equal") programs of daily life are functions of convictions about the people who have developed them and who pride themselves on having worked out an orderly process of life that minimizes tensions and maximizes the achievements of longstanding traditions.[9] Others stand by the principles outlined in the Bill of Rights and its reinforcement in civil rights' legislation, linking them together functionally to convictions about man and national process as stated in our charter documents.[10]

The list of domestic issues and underlying stories could be expanded almost indefinitely. But, for our present purposes, enough has been said to suggest both fields for and means of critical evaluation of the justifications alleged for both personal and social patterns of behavior in the matter of race relations. Behind the patterns we observe or hear about we always find one or more prominent storyteller whose account of the situation is motivating and influential because it has successfully created a coherent account of process-people-principles as relating to this particular domestic problem.

At this moment in history America finds itself deeply involved with other nations around the world. Most of these involvements are troublesome and at times even crucial, dealing as we do with alliances or confrontations between our nation and such diverse groups as our Western Allies and Russia, underdeveloped and developing nations like Africa, the countries of South America, and the so-called "banana republics," the Near and Far East, including China, Japan and Southeast Asia.

Behind the scenes of the daily news reports of some of our international activities, we can identify what commentators call the "Dulles doctrine," the "domino theory" about Southeast Asia, the NATO alliance, and a host of other justifications of our policies and procedures in dealing with the peoples and governments of the world.

In fact, experts in foreign affairs can trace out histories of the official stories, and changes in them, dating from our beginnings to the present. One such history distinguishes three periods of foreign policy thinking: (1) the first hundred years of our nation, its period of isolationism, (2) the next fifty years, a period of open-door, manifest destiny, and dollar diplomacy, (3) the period following World War II, the time of Communist containment policies.

Our early isolationist policies were built on a view of America as a fortress, a bastion of unique freedom for people who wanted to "live and let live." The process in which America was to thrive was that of isolating ourselves from other nations and being preoccupied with the tasks of building up the resources native to this land. It was, therefore, quite fitting that our government create principles suited to these views, and America followed policies of non-intervention and "no entangling alliances."

The story which succeeded this one recognized the world as the field of American expansion, the process being interpreted as one of reaching for our manifest destiny. The American people began to reinterpret themselves as a nation of creditors, holding the purse-strings of economic power as adequate leverage to keep us both free and developing. The principles that gave coherence and effectiveness to such views were policies of open-door trading and dollar diplomacy in winning friends and warding off enemies.

Since the Second World War, however, America is said to be following a view which interprets historical process as one of containing the Communist threat. Correspondingly, we have begun to view ourselves as the world's most effective enemy of Communism, holding aloft the torch of personal, political and economic freedom, and frequently seeing ourselves as a "God-fearing" people confronting the atheism of dialectical materialism. Thus, foreign policy has taken a strong military bent, providing "police forces," and even massive armies, as well as exercising economic and diplomatic sanctions on Communist countries and their sympathizers.

During this same period, however, we have witnessed an extensive and penetrating assessment of the morality and effectiveness of modern warfare. The critics of American involvement in Southeast Asia have brought the extended debate to a head in the 1960's, with both destructive and constructive suggestions about the management of our foreign affairs. Most of the anti-war criticism in the fifties and sixties centered around two distinct stories which had until then been justifying our behavior in international politics. The first is the so-called "just war theory," and the second is a modified form of pre-World-War II expansion policies (coupled with reinterpretations of what was needed for our own national security, as well as providing others with opportunities for self-determination in government).

There are any number of ways to critically evaluate the norms suggested in the just war theory, which according to some justifies too much.[11] Most discussions of the adequacy of this set of principles in modern warfare focus on the principles themselves. In accordance with our systems analogy, we might also suggest that these principles be scrutinized in terms of their coherence (or lack of same) with the related notions of people in community and the processes of maintaining justice and peace. A similar suggestion can also be made with respect to the stories undergirding policies of national defense and the definitions of national interest, especially when both of these matters find us deeply involved in the lives and destinies of nations all around the globe.

In one form or another all of these stories continue to motivate sectors of American foreign policy. While not necessarily operative in their most naive forms, subtle varieties of these same stories underpin much of what happens in the everyday decisions of our State Department and Pentagon. The student who wishes to take this area as one deserving special study can find numerous resources available, ranging from government documents to the studies of political analysts.[12]

While we cannot attempt to offer adequate guidelines for a critique of any or all of the aspects of U.S. foreign policy, we can suggest that you evaluate whatever aspect interests you by: (1) identifying the story behind the policy, (2) isolating the factors in it, (3) checking for incoherency in the functional inter-relationship of these factors. If we find the story wanting in coherence, then we can begin the work of reconstructing it, and can propose alternative stories in a manner to be detailed in the next section of this chapter.

INTERPERSONAL RELATIONS

If this is indeed to be the dawning of the Age of Aquarius, not all of the credit can be given to the stars. Much of it must also go to terrestrial interest in and efforts expended toward improving the relationships between people. We have been graced with abundant resources for understanding not only the difficulties associated with social processes like alienation, massification, and industrialization, but also the workings of some of the psychological processes in communication and friendship among human beings.

Mental illness.   From Sigmund Freud, Erich Fromm, Harry Stack Sullivan, and George H. Mead we have received sufficient prodding to reinterpret the psychic life of man and the institutionalized forms of life together. Martin Buber's *I and Thou* has become in one or another form the rallying cry and paradigm slogan for new principles of social and political life in the twentieth century.

What has happened can be termed a radical reinterpretation of the meaning of man, provoking equally fundamental reworkings of the principles guiding interpersonal relationships. One dramatic instance of the force of this revamping can be seen in the success of our century's story about mental health and illness. Less than one hundred years ago medical science had virtually no understanding of the nature of mental illness and we were the self-made victims of our misunderstandings of this disease, of our distorted and pejorative identifications of people afflicted with this problem, and our equally dehumanizing principles guiding public policies toward them. When we used to view the process of mental defects as one of biological or sociological heredity, we called the mentally ill "idiots, morons, crazy people" and created laws and institutions to rid society of their "bad influence" by whisking them off to asylums and prisons (such as Bedlam in England!).

However, in the 1960's we have federal programs establishing Community Mental Health Centers,[13] with some two hundred of them already in operation by 1969, providing short-term therapy (vs. the former extended periods of hospitalization). This is a step beyond what was already a significant procedural advance in the 1950's when over a half-million Americans were able to be treated in public mental health hospitals. We have moved from practices of jailing the sick to hospitalizing them, and gone one step further in providing short-term local aid, and all within the last few decades.

The point I would like to make here is that these practices are the consequence of new principles, which have sometimes been embodied in the form of laws. And the new principles are a result of a new conviction that mental health is a human right to be made available to everyone. But that judgment is not only a progressive step in federal law; it is also evidence of a new understanding of people, especially of those debilitated mentally. And this in turn is due to a century of medical, psychological and social understanding of the processes of being born and raised, adjusting to one's own self as well as to others, and the study of the pressures of constraint that play on people in society.

Consequently, a new story about mental health and illness can now be told. The factors have been transformed by new knowledge and can be related functionally in a new way to underpin a more enlightened public attitude and policy.

The family.[14]   What is a family for, or in what process is it engaged? What about the people in a family; how do you understand their personal and familial rights and obligations? By what principles would you organize and carry on the activities of family life?

These kinds of questions can be put to any statement made about family life as well as to any actual concrete example of a family in action. They are attempts to get answers about the key factors being used as the central features in any family-life story. The responses will be varied and curious. One family may be striving for moral and religious health, another for the full-flowering of all its members, and still another for wealth or success. Some will see its members as hierarchically structured in authorities, while others will try to consider each one, even the "little" ones, as persons "in their own right," and so on. Principles will vary to the greatest degree with very detailed lists of obligations in some, loose agreements about responsibilities in others, and endless variety in both of these general categories.

When critically evaluating a family plan or philosophy, the examiner can reasonably ask for either statements or evidence of coherence between the key factors. Inconsistencies can be pointed out-"if you are 'for' full personal development in all members of the family, why do you have house rules which prescribe an after-dinner hike for all?" Revealing such inconsistencies may not only be helpful to a particular family, but may also help rework the basic story of family life as it is passed on through its children.

When the coherence of the factors in the family-life story is critically examined, it is usually also extended to all of the relationships prior to formalized family living. It provokes consideration of issues like dating, courtship, and premarital intimacies, so that extramarital and paramarital relationships are also called before the bench of assessment to ascertain the coherence of their stories. By saying this, however, I do not wish to imply that the discovery of incoherence in any or all of these stories is in itself sufficient warrant to immediately change particular customs or patterns. There are, often enough, other and very important reasons for continuing along the customary path until better stories can be developed and proven useful. By pointing to possible inconsistencies in family stories I merely intend to note that, if the justifying story is inconsistent, it ought to be revised, or otherwise stand the danger of reasonable rebellion irrationally brought against its inconsistency.

In such a complex and emotionally-charged matter as family life, we would be foolish to consider any one evaluative criterion as sufficient unto itself. Hence, what is suggested here as the criterion of a good story should be taken as just one more, possibly helpful, standard by which to examine and evaluate what we stand for and do in this important area of social life.

Love. Before concluding this section on interpersonal relations we ought to mention one of our overriding stories which animates a large part of our national effort in living well with others. And this is the story told about the meaning of love.[15] Erich Fromm claims that Americans have a great deal to say on this topic, but that this is a symptom of the absence rather than the presence of love in life in this country, based on the conviction that we tend to talk most about what we most desperately need.[16]

There is certainly no national story of love to which we all pledge allegiance, but there are widely communicated stories of love by which we are all just as certainly influenced. These, then, can become the object of criticism, factor-analysis and testing, using our rule of coherence. The most prominent stories of love inviting such criticism are the "being loved" story, that of "falling in love," and those emphasizing the physical and romantic side of lovemaking. Each of these types of stories contains some implicit or explicit statement about the people who get involved in the loving process, and the kinds of rules which ought to regulate their mutual behavior. Critical assessment of love stories has been one of the national pastimes for experts from all areas concerned with man's behavior in society. Every sort of normative model of love, from the religious to the psychological, is offered as "the" norm. But even these are stories to be tested by the same criteria we would use in evaluating the more common and widely motivating models of love.

Hence, it seems entirely appropriate to suggest that our systems analogy be tried in the area of love stories, and that students who wish to get some further insight into this pervasive social interest do so by identifying the three factors and evaluating their functional coherence. If you find one of these stories very helpful in its recommended principles, yet having a very twisted notion of people, you have found incoherence and a beginning for possible improvement in the story and the behavior depending upon it.

BASIC PHILOSOPHIES

In addition to the stories which justify specific areas of behavior in particular sectors of national life, we can point to larger stories like that of love and some commonly accepted philosophies that act as stories for the general populace. We usually can agree that some such story is told about the purpose of our nation as "an experiment in democracy." We do not hesitate to identify the Constitution and its amendments as the principles factor in this story, and willingly recount the process and people views of its drafters. Yet most of the time, this is done in an uncritical spirit, praising the wisdom and courage of our founding fathers.

In the interests of historical accuracy we would have to admit that our national philosophy has gone through several revisions. And, it seems accurate to say that these revisions have not left the basic story completely intact, but have, in fact, reworked it into successively different stories, whose continuity with the original can be traced but not without also acknowledging the disappearance of the original as actually operative and motivating in today's society.

In fact, there is evidence indicating that the original story in the Continental Congress was itself not unanimously accepted by all Americans at that time. And so, one might wonder why we even attempt to discuss generalized stories which, when examined carefully, were never held generally at all. It was concern about this which prompted me to put this issue last, only after having discussed particular stories about very specific aspects of national life. For, I do not see the value in considering the general philosophy of life held by all Americans since there not only does not seem to be such a thing, but also since efforts to identify one seem artificial and primarily interested in debating or refuting it. If, then, the point of these constructs is one of creating straw men for easy demolition, it should not be given a great deal of attention in this study.

However, we can admit that these generalized stories have some value in that they get us thinking. We can be challenged to thought about stories that promote a view of history as a forward march toward an ever better life, an unswerving line of progress in which things are getting "better and better." Philosophers, social theorists, and ordinary people would like to challenge this view and confront it with a cyclical interpretation that admits of crests and troughs in history, if not actual cycles of recurrence.[17]

Similarly, it is useful to think about the process of the cosmos, to rethink philosophies attributing too much autonomy to man and his dominion over his environment. Principles and behaviors built on such assumptions are presently being criticized for creating havoc with the environment and the ecological balance of the planet earth, as well as possibly disturbing other planets.

There is some value too in challenging the factors and functional coherence in nihilistic philosophies which oppose progress illusions with dreams of emptiness (the *nihil* or *neant*), and schemes of principles which effectively paralyze the human will.

In short, the scrutiny of general philosophical stories is a worthwhile and valuable exercise in the art of criticism. But it is of little help if it is

applied glibly to all areas and peoples in America. To say that we understand all of our actual social and political stories when we have scrutinized the
Constitution or the philosophy of John Locke is not at all true. The only
really fruitful scrutiny is the one that carefully searches out the story that is
actually functioning in some particular policy or behavior and examines *that*.

The Art of Construction

The purpose of what has been said thus far in this chapter is one of both
stimulating interest in socio-political stories and suggesting some guidelines
for assessing them. The pursuit of this interest and technique will be of some
assistance in developing a more refined critical skill, but critical capabilities
must also be paralleled by constructive skills. We must be as skillful with the
needle and thread as we are with the scalpel, or the cancer removed will
be quickly replaced by an equally destructive illness. Therefore, our attention must now turn to the task of reworking socio-political stories and providing alternatives for those we find unsatisfactory and incoherent.

To begin with we shall consider a large-scale reconstruction model
developed by the sociologist Pitirim Sorokin. During the thirties and forties
Sorokin was trying to identify and chart socio-cultural trends in what he
called the "Euro-American Culture," and published his results in a four-
volume work entitled *Social and Cultural Dynamics*.[18] Subsequent to that work
he lectured widely on the same topic and produced another version of his
thesis in *The Crisis of Our Age*.[19]

Sorokin developed a typology of logically integrated cultures, and divided
them into two main types, the *sensate* and the *ideational* or *idealistic*, adding
cautions that they are not necessarily found as pure types, but merely represent the predominant strains in every type of culture.[20] The *sensate* recognizes
only the sensory as real, emphasizes flux and evolution, and aims at satisfying
the physical needs of man by modifying or exploiting the external world.
The *ideational* type is a culture integrated around notions of reality as ever-
lasting and immaterial, in which human needs and goals are viewed as
primarily spiritual, and the satisfaction of those needs is had by modifying
one's self rather than the environment.[21]

With this scheme in mind we can begin to understand Sorokin's conviction that we are witnessing the end of a six-hundred year reign of sensate
culture in the western world, and are beginning to see signs that tomorrow's
ideational culture is dawning. This process gives him reason for hope and
creates a pleasant prospect for the renewal rather than the collapse of western
culture. But man must be tamed and humanized in order to realize this
prospect. He must bring himself and his lusts under control. Sorokin considers
this impossible without a system of absolute or perennial values, which assure
self-control and firm up the integrating ideas of an ideational culture.[22]

What he has sketched out is an excellent example of the art of construction. It tells a new and coherent story about the large picture of western civilization, contains the process-people-principles factors in tight functional relationships, and has been highly motivating for many people in the fifties. As a story, it looks to the future, and makes a calculated and reasonable guess about where we are heading and what we will need when we arrive there.

Just as we can critically evaluate the stories currently in vogue, so too can we judge a story about future prospects. We should, therefore, expect that the guidelines suggested for the art of criticism will continue to be employed in the constructive models of future behavior. However, before we can intelligently assess Sorokin's suggestion, or any other, we must have a better understanding of what he and others are doing when they suggest what may or ought to happen in the future. We must have a firm basis in the guidelines of the art of construction before we can evaluate such work.

While some would find in Sorokin's story a species of determinism,[23] there can be no doubt about the insatiable hunger of contemporary man for some such story. The mood of the present is one of increased attention to the future. This mood is born of a dual conviction that recognizes that western culture has been in a state of decline and that man is faced with the imperative of not allowing the future to become the product of chance or arbitrary will. Not all will agree on the signs that indicate a decline but all will testify to an increased iconoclasm and nihilism toward the traditional images of truth, goodness and beauty in the western world. While some may puzzle over the degree of man's capacity to manipulate his future, none would be so reckless as to forego all efforts to shape it as carefully as we can. There is, then, a basis of agreement that something is happening and its outcome is partly our responsibility. And from that common ground efforts radiate in numerous directions, including socio-political forecasting, "anticipatory designing,"[24] process philosophies and theologies, matured utopian thinking and revolutionary consciousness.

The question arises as to precisely where along this spectrum humanistic contributions might be made. Does humanism in the West connote traditionalism, the conservation and reiteration of the stories and values out of the heritage of the past? It surely has, and a similar view reappears in romantic efforts to set the clock back and bring about a rebirth of some former age considered golden or classical. The present mood rightly rejects this rear-view approach, and thereby rejects with it a humanism which promotes the archaeological resurrection of dreams past. The question remains, then, whether humanism *can* be pertinent to the present and its hopes for the future. Some will rightly remind us that the romantic form of humanism mentioned above ignores the more positive side of the humanistic contribution. They can point with pride to the forward-looking visions of poets, painters, musicians and religionists, their dreams of the future as well as their personal contributions in trying to make them come true.

With this opinion I would side and state my belief in man's capacity for constructing positive images of the future. I would acknowledge some signs of a falling-off of purposeful awareness of the future, as well as the crippled state of religious, aesthetic, humanistic and idealistic awareness.[25] In the face of this, I would hope in order to try, remembering that it is not necessary to succeed in order to persevere,[26] and would stand with the conviction that man can create purposeful, vital, and inspiring images of the future. With these we can begin to break the death grip of present dilemmas and free ourselves to think about and act for the future. This, it seems, is the role and obligation of the humanist. He can and must reconstruct the stories of human life in such a way that they can become the life blood of socio-political and cultural life in America and around the planet.

The art of construction stands, then, on a conviction similar to that of H.G. Wells, who said:

> I believe that the deliberate direction of historical study and of economic and social study toward the future, and an increasing reference, a deliberate and courageous reference, to the future in moral and religious discussion, would be enormously stimulating and enormously profitable to our intellectual life.*

And, I would add, it can be equally profitable to all areas of human behavior which use stories to justify and undergird their policies and practices.

To return now to the story told by Sorokin in our example at the beginning of this section on the art of construction, we might say that his purpose was more like that of the humanist than that of the social scientist (or perhaps he should be called a "humanistic social scientist"). He was surely forecasting and estimating the laws and effects of social and cultural changes. He was also, it seems to me, telling a story of what he would like to see happen, of what would be beneficial to mankind, namely, its passing from a sensate to an ideational type of culture. He told this story by means of a *model* which he had adopted. By *model* we ought not to understand the traditional humanist notion of an artist's model or an ethical model for emulation and imitation. Rather, we ought to understand that model here means an "artificial construct to represent or imitate reality," a "fiction" in the root sense of the latin verb *fingo* (that is, "what is imagined or shaped"). If a model (such as an image or story) is motivating, it will give rise to sufficient effort

* Bertrand de Jouvenel, *The Art of Conjecture*, (New York: Basic Books, Inc., Publishers, 1967), p. 47.

to bring it into actuality, and therein lies the as yet unexplained but terribly important area of work that lies ahead for humanists and social scientists in consort with each other.[27] But it also accounts for the fact that many have found and continue to find Sorokin's story appealing. What he has done might be called conjecture by some, and dismissed as having a pejorative connotation. However, we need not capitulate to this interpretation and can try to see what value, if any, lies in conjecturing about the future.

Conjecture about the future is cultivated and prized by many today, including the research foundation called the "Futuribles" in Paris, under the direction of Bertrand de Jouvenel. This group has dedicated itself to instigating and stimulating efforts at social and political forecasting. De Jouvenel's personal interests, of late, have focused on an attempt to understand how the activity of forecasting proceeds, that is, to analyze *post factum* what people were doing when they framed their models of future behavior.[28] He claims that we are daily transforming our models into future realities, and that forecasting is simply an effort to improve on this activity. It is *not* a case of *foreknowledge*, or claiming certainty for our knowledge of what will happen. It is, rather, a case of *foresight*, or a provident concern to act well and prudently.[29] The demand for such provision has increased exponentially in modern times and the recipe-knowledge of former times serves us poorly as we confront the entirely novel problems of our day. At best, recipe-knowledge serves only to save us the effort of foresight; at its worst, it turns energy-conserving routines into reactionary familial, social, and political orders. Consequently, the present mood focuses on *futuribles*, those things that are *likely to happen*, (that is, strong probabilities) and tries to gauge what is desirable as well. For when the probable and the desirable nearly coincide, it seems that we try to bend the course of events to bring the probable closer to the desirable.[30]

Therefore, in estimating the probabilities of certain futuribles we must try to identify what we intend, that is, to what we will stretch or strive. What is it that now exercises an attraction to me? How able is it to mobilize my energies in pursuit of it? In short, what story will I work toward and help to bring into actuality? We are frequently reminded that the success of any project is founded upon people's attitudes and behavior, and the thesis of this study is that these two elements are directly related to ethical stories out of which we sort the principles factor as guidelines for adjusting both attitudes and behavior. For this reason, we now return to the main point of this section, to reiterate the fact that we presently stand in need of better stories in several key areas of the American and international scenes.

What would seem helpful, at this point, is a series of suggestions about some of the imaginative stories being proposed today. To maintain both clarity and a parallel with what has been said in "the art of criticism" we shall put these proposals in the categories used earlier in this chapter.

DOMESTIC ISSUES

Robert Theobald, one of the most stimulating of contemporary British socio-economists, has written and lectured widely on the changes America will have to undergo if it is to avert socio-economic collapse. A series of his essays is collected in *An Alternative Future for America*, which aims its sights at two presently critical domestic issues, namely, basic economic security and education. His critical evaluations of governmental mishandling of welfare and the reactionary habits of most mentors in higher education are matched with imaginative stories of guaranteed income and totally reorganized systems of learning. Behind the present systems he finds a view of man as a being who can be shaped, coerced and fitted to arbitrary but traditional social norms. The alternative, which he finds more congruous with the emphases of the American tradition, would rest on an optimistic and trusting notion of the free individual.[31]

Projected trends and tales about the future of education abound. Many see the library on the rise in the form of a central data bank, and the consequent decline of the classroom. Some predict students will spend most of their time in independent study, and may even follow college curricula without ever leaving home. If the physical boundaries of the university campus disappear, any number of roles will have to change, and with them, of course, attitudes and practices presently in vogue. Consequently, many readers should be able to find in this area a fertile field for seeding with new and well-told stories.[32]

Out of the dilemmas of race relations in our country there arise many hopeful as well as frightening stories of what may and should happen in this area. One very provocative picture portrays the tragic side of world process, joins with it a realistic if not very optimistic understanding of man, and leads to principles that would considerably alter many present practices. The general outline of this story is as follows: Perhaps there is but one branch of the human race which has really paid the price of life in its suffering—the black branch! Because they have been deeply seared by oppression, it may well be the case that only the black men are open and sensitive enough to lead the non-white and suffering masses of men into true community. Perhaps these people will trust no others but those who have truly felt life's pain and suffering.[33]

This is certainly not a pleasant prospect for many Americans. But it brings something important to our attention, namely, the question whether or not all stories constructed for the future need to be joyful, pleasant and optimistic. It may well be the case that the tragic is too often excluded in our constructions, and, therefore, needs reassertion as a characteristic element in all stories about human behavior. This could be pursued further by attending to the popularity of *The Man of La Mancha*[34] and considering what the story of Don Quixote would be without its deft blending of tragi-comic elements.

AMERICA AMONG THE NATIONS

One of the most enticing new stories to interest Americans is one suggesting non-violence as a possible strategy in world affairs. In the face of an unprecedented capacity to kill off all human beings several times over, some regard non-violence as the most effective and most promising defense policy.[35] The popularity of India's Gandhi has risen proportionately during this time and interest in his philosophy and tactics have reached new levels.[36] The belief that war is a normal extension of diplomacy is being challenged and suggestions are being made that Japan's adoption of a peaceful, non-military policy might turn the tide of foreign-policy dilemmas in the Far East.[37]

Non-violence is by far the most mind-stretching proposal for American thinking on our role among the nations. But it is not the only significant proposal of an alternative story to quicken the pace of improving world affairs. Other suggestions include the opinion that world civilization is shifting focal points to the East, and that, culturally speaking, the prospect is for a world civilization cast in the Oriental mold. The West, it claims, has served its role of stewardship and must now pass on the torch to the Asian world and prepare itself for some future form of social and political union with Asia.[38]

A slightly different story is told by William O. Douglas who builds on the assumptions that men want to survive, but are unruly and overreaching, and, therefore, both personally and in groups called nations, require a rule of law. U.S. foreign policy in Asia should, therefore, aim at helping Asians set up and guarantee national boundaries, tribunals and means for adjudicating disputes.[39]

However, some other proposals see stories about nationalism and national sovereignty as the principal culprits in the breakdown of modern peace-making efforts, and suggest fresher visions of a new world culture, an amalgam of all men pledged to invest their resources in a single world republic with a single destiny.[40] This proposal would stand on three founding notions, namely, (1) the unity of mankind, (2) the freedom of the person, and (3) the community of wealth.[41] It would go beyond the federalist suggestions of earlier "world constitutions,"[42] bypassing the cooperation they require from existing sovereign nations, and would act outside these present frameworks by cultivating myths, legends, martyrs, heroes and symbols of a new world-mind. The *coup d'etat* would thereby be replaced with dreaming the *coup de monde*. Its challenge would be to bring on a moral, intellectual, and psychic revolution that would ransom all existing national structures from their present state of bankruptcy.[43]

There are any number of further suggestions for more positive and creative foreign affairs policies. They can easily be found through further reading in this area, can be evaluated by using the rule of coherence, and can be improved through personal effort expended in reconstructing them. The plans mentioned here are simply suggested as those resources presently familiar to this writer, who hopes his readers will find others by following up the pointers provided here.

As we move through the seventies and forward, the issues that formed the bases of the "new morality" discussions will probably wane through either lack of pressing concern or failure to be meaningful confrontations with established stories and codes of sexual ethics. Premarital and extra-marital sexuality will probably be less cogent issues than those of the corporate family, the intentional community and the issues that will be raised as we enter the days when abortion and genetic control will be more widely considered as necessary means of handling social problems.

Therefore, the student of future possible stories about life together would do well to know some of the reconstructions being suggested at this time. Among these, the novels of Robert Rimmer stand out as both captivating and provocative.[44] They sum up much of today's psychological thought and project, in the form of the novel, some experiments in what may prove to be viable alternatives to monogamous marriage. They merit the attention of anyone interested in this area both because of their popularity and the challenges they present for evaluating reconstructed stories of family life.

As an extension of Rimmer's *Proposition 31* our attention could also be directed to experiments in communal living. Intentional communities and communes are cropping up around the country and injecting new life into former attempts at corporate living. Some may want to either investigate or promote these forms of life together, and will find the area of proposals growing quite rapidly in recent years.

However, biological manipulation of man promises to be one of the most sensitive areas of stories and theories about interpersonal relations. Within five or more years, for example, scientists predict we will have the technological capacity to regulate sexual desire, chemically or mechanically. Storage of eggs and sperm, artificial insemination with the sperm of "great men," and the genetic control of large populations are also in the realm of probability by the year 2000.[45]

Advances such as these and the decisions about how we should employ them will be aimless, and perhaps catastrophic to human love, unless many creative minds begin applying themselves to the task of constructing new models of sexual love, family life, and the rights of human beings. If we have the opportunity to control the genetic structure of heredity, should we use it? If we do, what kinds of people would we want—a society of geniuses and "great men," or a variety sufficiently diverse to make life interesting? Who will decide? On what models will they base their decisions? Which human types make life more pleasant, efficient, spiritual, or whatever we conclude we want? In answering these questions and making proposals, it will be most helpful to use the model of a system in order to draw out the implications of brilliant flashes of insight.

BASIC PHILOSOPHIES

It seems there will always be a place for the more general stories about life in America, or, for that matter, about life on the planet Earth, in its galaxy, or in the solar system. Several current reconstructions of such stories merit our attention and perhaps our endorsement.

There are suggestions of an historical nature promoting the notion of man as one of unending potentiality, with the future seen as one of open-ended possibility.[46] Others focus on the physical, biological and evolutionary processes of the universe and try to persuade us to consider the goals of cosmic consciousness.[47] Still others offer suggestions for humanizing technology, including the mobilization of a new constituency of conscience in the form of a national movement.[48]

These are but a few of the varied suggestions in currency today. Those with interest in the value of these and similar stories will find no lack of materials available to jog their imaginations and occasion the telling of still better tales.

Concluding Cautions and Suggestions

Which, if any, of these above proposals will catch on and lead to a new day depends largely on how feasible they are. Dreaming of the future has long been in a state of disrepute due to the snobbish idealism of visionaries who refused to distinguish between the purely possible and the truly probable. By flaunting the general need for psychological equilibrium, some utopian thinking has proceeded on the assumption that "the practical man" does not have sufficient resources to stir himself in the attaining of grandiose schemes. But the practical man has this much going for him, namely, his skill in weeding out the improbable or unattainable. He can and will zone off what lies outside the limits of likely human behavior and will not be moved by what appears to him as incapable of implementation. Therefore, many good stories and plans will be ignored and rejected due to their unattainability. Hence, it is worth remembering that it makes no sense to tell socio-political stories which are necessarily restricted to giving stimulus only to one's self or one's "in-group." This would do little to benefit the characteristically communal problem areas highlighted in this chapter. Hence, one caution about constructing new stories is a reminder to keep the audience in mind, and to scale stories to the range of what is considered attainable.

A second caution concerns the difference between myth-making and myth-mongering. "Synthetic" stories make many people uneasy, especially if they prove to be useful in the hands of power structures. One thinks readily of the myth-mongering done during the era of the second world war in Germany, Japan and the U.S.A. and becomes wary of stories that can be used as propaganda by dictators, however benevolent they may be. Hence, to suggest reconstructing stories for social consumption puts many on their guard and raises the specter of the dehumanizing propaganda techniques common to myth-mongers. Myth-making is, however, a human activity, which, when gone astray, leads to the aforementioned abuses. How then keep it on the track and moving in the direction of furthering man's capacity and dignity? Clearly, one criterion would be the degree to which any story helps bring the best out of us. Stories that appeal to our less worthy emotions, or fears and hatreds, would certainly be suspect. Those that portray our usefulness in the service of abstractions like the gross national product would likewise be undeserving. Only those stories which ask us to transcend our limitations and invite our participation in wider areas of social and planetary welfare deserve our attention. Stories that call for improving life together irrespective of national, ethnic and religious differences would also qualify as truly helpful. Other characteristics can be mentioned as well, but these are a few of the more prominent ones to be kept in mind as we search for new models of human living.

A final comment can now be made more in the form of a caution than a constructive guideline. If man needs stories told to him, must religion alone be trusted to tell him the truly meaningful and ennobling ones, or can others do it as well? At this point in history, many would put the question otherwise, asking if religion has not already ceased functioning in this role and been replaced by others doing a much better job. Many will grant that religious traditions have provided mankind with some of its most vital and persistent symbols, and have triggered a transformation of vision and unleashing of creativity over the centuries.[49] We are, however, hard pressed at this point in western history because much of our religious tradition has been demystified or secularized, if not altogether ignored.[50] Consequently, many will rightly wonder how to approach the present and future of story-telling. They will have to decide whether or not they ought to rework, update, and make traditional religious stories more relevant. It will be clear that several alternatives exist, along a spectrum from entirely new religious stories to none at all. In the middle ranges, moving toward the latter pole, judgments will have to be made about the extent to which elements of religious insight and value will be employed.

The substance of these concluding remarks is obviously tentative, but there are few things of which we can be certain and these have already been pointed out in the course of this study. What we do not yet know is precisely where or how religious ethics will continue to be helpful to man. The caution given here is merely this writer's way of saying that religious ethics may prove to be more than a mere model of a good story, but that this must be decided by those who tell and hear the meaning-making fictions of man in the twentieth century.

STUDY QUESTIONS

1. Critically evaluate some readily available code of behavior (student regulations, city ordinances on loitering). If you should find the system functionally coherent, but disagree with one of the factors, can you restate that factor and still preserve the system's coherence?

2. Choose an example of federal foreign-affairs policy and critically examine it on the basis of the inferred rules of coherence.

3. Consider the basic philosophy of "Zuckerkandlism" (Cf. Joseph P. Lyford interviews R. M. Hutchins, "Living Without Guilt", in *The Center Magazine*, Volume III, number 1, January, 1970, p. 2 ff.) and test its coherence, as well as your sense of humor.

4. Try to construct a model of a language system whose principles uphold "continuous ferment" and continuous recreation of one's psychic and social structures.

5. Imagine yourself in a totally new environment (say, for example, married and shopping with your spouse in a sperm and egg storage bank). How do you regard yourself? In what kind of life-theater are you living?

6. Take some future-oriented story of life near the year 2000. Improve one of its factors more to your liking, and then determine what must also be changed in the other factors to preserve the system's coherence.

NOTES

1. Cf. Winston L. King's schema of viewpoints in footnote 1 of preface.

2. Attributed to John Dewey ("My Pedagogic Creed" of 1897), cited by R. M. Hutchins, "Permanence and Change" in *The Center Magazine*, vol. I, no. 6 (September, 1968), p. 2. Cf. also Daniel Bell, *The Reforming of General Education* (New York: Columbia University Press, 1966), pp. 8, 156–58.

3. Cf. *Introduction to Natural Science* by Parsegian *et al.*, Part One, c. 6, pp. 185 ff., esp. p. 202.

4. You might also pursue this matter in the form found in the book *In Search of America*, ed. by Huston Smith (Englewood Cliffs, N.J.: Prentice Hall, Inc., 1959). Note: This work is the result of a thirty-two program television series prepared for National Educational Television. The first sixteen programs were devoted to the values currently (1950's!) animating U.S. life, and the second set of sixteen sought to identify the sense of the direction to be taken in the future (cf. preface, p. vii). The events of national life in the sixties make it imperative to both expand and modify much of what is said in this book, but the problems and quality of the participants make it a work still valuable as a starting place for those who are still new to critical examinations of the problem areas treated.

5. *op. cit.*, Part II, p. 45 ff.

6. Cf. The Woodrow Wilson—Theodore Roosevelt campaign and Roosevelt's ridiculing of Wilson, calling him "the professor"; cf. Smith, *op. cit.*, p. 95. Cf. also the campaign oratory of George Wallace in the 1960's with the frequent references to "pseudo-intellectuals," and his appeal to the lower ranges of America's middle class, riddled as it is with fears of the advance of the Blacks, Communists, and bureaucracy in Washington.

7. Cf. the differing policies of the HEW Secretary (especially their emphases on key areas in education) in the Kennedy Administration, that of Johnson and Nixon. Cf. also Samuel Houston Johnson's comments on his brother Lyndon who disliked most of Kennedy's cabinet, excepting Rusk, whom Johnson admired (cf. *Look* magazine **33**: 24, Dec. 2, 1969, p. 60). In sharp contrast, however, Sam Johnson quotes LBJ turning down the intellectualistic Adlai Stevenson as a possible running-mate in the 1964 convention (cf. *Look*, **33**: 25, Dec. 16, 1969, p. 44). Similarly, when reminded of Senator J. William Fulbright, LBJ " . . . occasionally reminded people that Harry Truman had called Fulbright 'an overeducated sonofabitch'," and claimed that Fulbright was " . . . naive and inept in the day-to-day maneuvering inside the Senate ('Hell, he can't even park a bicycle')" (cf. *op. cit., loc. cit.*, p. 51).

8. Smith, *op. cit.*, pp. 54–64. Cf. also separatist assumptions (*both* black and white) in Thomas F. Pettigrew, "Racially Separate or Together" in *Journal of Social Issues*, 25: 1, pp. 43–69, esp. 46–48, and Joseph S. Himes, "The Function of Racial Conflict" in *Social Forces*, **45**: 1 (Sept., 1966), pp. 1–10. Cf. also new types of ego-identity through new images obtained through social confrontation in Frederic Solomon and Jacob R. Rishman, "Youth and Social Action: II. Action and Identity Formation in the First Student Sit-in Demonstration" in *Journal of Social Issues* **20**: 2, pp. 36–45, esp. p. 36 ff.

9. Cf. William J. Simmons, "Race in America: The Conservative Stand" in Smith, *op. cit.*, p. 54 ff; cf. also the platform of the Black Muslims in *In Their Own Behalf: Voice from the Margin*, editors: C. H. McCagley, J. K. Skipper, M. Lefton (New York: Appleton-Century-Crofts, 1968), p. 174 ff.

10. Cf. Harry Ashmore, "Race in America: A Southern Moderate's View", in Smith, *op. cit.*, p. 45 ff.

11. Cf. Donald A. Wells, "The 'Just War' Justifies Too Much" in *Philosophy for a New Generation*, ed. Bierman and Gould (New York: The Macmillan Company,

1968), pp. 218–230; Cf. also *Morality and Modern Warfare*, William Nagle, Editor, (Baltimore: Helicon, 1960).

12. Confer the suggested readings in *In Search of America*, Part I, and the "Ethics and Foreign Policy Series" pamphlets of the Council on Religion and International Affairs, 170 E. 64th St., New York, New York, 10021.

13. Cf. 1963 act of federal government.

14. Cf. Margaret Mead, "The Family" in Smith, *op. cit.*, p. 116 ff: cf. also Ruth Anshen, ed., *The Family: Its Function and Destiny* (New York: Harper & Row, Publishers, 1959).

15. Cf. Erich Fromm, "Love in America" in Smith, *op. cit.*, p. 123 ff., and his book *The Art of Loving* (New York: Harper & Row, Publishers, 1956), cf. also Denis de Rougemont, *Love in the Western World* (New York: Doublèday & Company, Inc., 1957).

16. Fromm, *op. cit.*, *loc. cit.*

17. Cf. Jules Karlin, *Man's Behavior* (New York: The Macmillan Company, 1967), Part V "Man and History", p. 499 ff., esp. p. 551 ff, on the challenges of cyclical theories from Giambattista Vico through Oswald Spengler to Arnold Toynbee.

18. (Boston: Porter Sargent, Publisher, 1957), a one-volume abridged version of the four-volume 1937 original.

19. (New York: E. P. Dutton, 1941), a modified form of the 1941 Lowell Institute lectures on "The Twilight of Sensate Culture."

20. Cf. *Social and Cultural Dynamics*, pp. 622–28.

21. *ibid.*

22. *ibid.*, cf. also *The Crisis of Our Age*, c. IX "The Disintegration of Sensate Culture: The Roots of the Crisis and the Way Out", pp. 298–326. Note: These values are necessarily associated with religion and promoted by new or renewed religious visions.

23. Fred L. Polak, *The Image of the Future* (Enlightening the Past, Orientating the Present, Forecasting the Future), two volumes, (New York: Oceana Publications, Inc., 1961), vol. II, p. 350–52.

24. Cf. the work of R. Buckminster Fuller.

25. Cf. Daniel Bell's *The End of Ideology* (New York, 1965).

26. A stoic axiom.

27. Cf. Polak's comment on the need for understanding the "theory and dynamics of image formation, and field studies of current images of the future in action," in *op. cit.*, vol. II, p. 366; cf. also c. 4 of this study on *li* and *jen* in Confucius. Note: interest is building in this study of images, in the form of a new field of behavioral science called "eiconics".

28. Bertrand de Jouvenel, *The Art of Conjecture:* cf. also structural-functional analysis of the prerequisites for "future systems" in Amitai Ezioni, *Studies in Social Change* (New York: Holt, Rinehart and Winston, Inc., 1966).

29. Cf. Thomas Aquinas' thoughts on the importance of foresight for the virtue of prudence; cf. his *Summa Theologiae*, II-II, q. 49, a.6; cf. also Josef Pieper, *Prudence* (New York: Pantheon Books, Inc., 1969). p. 36.

30. de Jouvenel, *op. cit.*, p. 19.

31. Cf. Preface to Theobald's *An Alternative Future for America*, written by Noel McInnis and Kendall College students (Evanston, Illinois).

32. Cf. resources in *Campus 1980: The Shape of the Future in American Higher Education*, ed. by Alvin C. Eurich (New York: Delacorte Press, 1968). Cf. also *The Futurist*, III: 6 (December, 1969) pp. 149–53, George B. Leonard, *Education and Ecstasy* (New York: Delacorte Press, 1968), *Philosophy for a New Generation*, esp. c. II "Philosophy and Ideology of the University", pp. 33–87, and a most stimulating new title *Worlds in the Making: Probes for Students of the Future*, Mary Jane Dunstan and Patricia Garlan, editors (Englewood Cliffs, N.J.: Prentice Hall, Inc., 1970), especially Chap. 18 "Education-Evolution."

33. Vincent Harding, "The Afro-American Past," in *New Theology No. 6*, ed. M. Marty, and D. Peerman (New York: The Macmillan Company, 1969), pp. 167–77; the passage in question is found on p. 176. Note: this article appeared originally in *Motive* magazine, April, 1968. Cf. also Talcott Parsons, Kenneth B. Clark, *The Negro American* (Boston: Houghton Mifflin Company, 1966).

34. Cf. the musical by that title, a reworking of Miguel De Cervantes Saavedra's novel *Don Quixote*.

35. Cf. Gordon Zahn, *An Alternative to War*, pamphlet in the "Ethics and Foreign Policy Series" of the Council on Religion and International Affairs, 1963.

36. Cf. the centenary of Gandhi's birth in 1969 and Erik Erikson's *Gandhi's Truth* (New York: W. W. Norton & Company, Inc., 1969).

37. Cf. J. W. Fulbright "A New Realism for an Outworn Rationality" in *Asian Dilemma* (Santa Barbara: Center, 1969); An Occasional Paper from the Center for the Study of Democratic Institutions, vol. II, no. 5, Oct., 1969, pp. 217–19.

38. Cf. Harvey Wheeler, "Asiatic Union", *ibid.*, pp. 219–26.

39. Cf. his "Recipe for Survival: An Untried Approach in An Unprecedented Age" in *Asian Dilemma*, pp. 227–29.

40. W. Warren Wagar, "Toward the City of Man" in *The Center Magazine*, I: 6 (September, 1968), pp. 33–41.

41. *ibid.*

42. Cf. the so-called "Chicago Draft" of *A Constitution For the World* (Santa Barbara: Center for the Study of Democratic Institutions, 1965). Note: The first publication of this document was called *A Preliminary Draft of a World Constitution* (Chicago: University of Chicago Press, 1948). It was redone in 1965 after the "*Pacem in Terris* Convocation" in New York, and the San Francisco celebration of the twentieth anniversary of the United Nations. Its basic rationale is one based on a conviction that western civilization has moved from the city state to the nation, must now move from national governments to regional governments, in order to eventually move from regional polities to a world republic.

43. Similar suggestions will be found in Erich Fromm's *Revolution of Hope* (New York: Bantam Books, Inc., 1968). p. 147 ff.

44. Cf. his books: *The Harrad Experiment*, *The Rebellion of Yale Marratt* and *Proposition 31*.

45. Cf. Gordon Rattray Taylor's *The Biological Time Bomb* (New York: New American Library, 1968).

46. Cf. Harvey Cox, "Ernst Bloch and 'The Pull of the Future'" in *New Theology No. 5*, Marty-Peerman, editors (New York: The Macmillan Company, 1968). Cf. also Part II: "The Theology of Hope-Enthusiastic Words" in *op. cit.*, p. 79 ff.

47. Cf. Teilhard de Chardin *The Phenomenon of Man*, (New York: Harper and Row, Publishers, 1961).

48. Cf. Erich Fromm, *The Revolution of Hope*.

49. Cf. Ninian Smart, *The Religious Experience of Mankind* (New York: Charles Scribner's Sons, 1968), Ralph Ross *Symbols and Civilization*, (New York: Harcourt Brace Jovanovich, Inc., 1962), and Marx Wartofsky, "Telos and Technique: Models As Modes of Action" in *Planning for Diversity and Choice*, Stanford Anderson, ed. (Cambridge, Mass.: MIT Press, 1968), p. 259 ff.

50. Cf. Peter Berger, *The Sacred Canopy* (New York: Doubleday & Company, Inc., 1967), Harvey Cox, *The Secular City* (New York: The Macmillan Company, 1965), William Hamilton, and Thomas Altizer, *Radical Theology and the Death of God* (Indianapolis: The Bobbs-Merrill Co., Inc., 1966), and Gabriel Vahanian, *The Death of God* (New York: George Braziller, Inc., 1961).

Appendix
Four Traditions
in Christian Ethics

GENERAL QUESTION	PARTICULAR ANSWERS	BIBLICAL TEXTS MOST OFTEN CITED	PRINCIPAL PROCESS SYMBOLS	CHRIST IS...	PEOPLE ARE...	PRINCIPLES ADVISE US TO...	PRINCIPAL PROPONENTS	REPRESENTATIVES IN RECENT DEBATES
"What difference does Christ make in the Christian's Moral Life?"	1 HE IS THE LORD, WHO IS THE CREATOR AND REDEEMER	"Logos" texts where the preexistence and cosmic function of Christ is stressed	CREATION AND REDEMPTION	LORD, WHO MAKES, AND REMAKES	Not autonomous, but "in relation"; the true relationship is given in creation, known only in redemption. Thus, man is a "partaker" who is "against" God, but, in Christ, God is "for" man	Be critical of all human ethics, giving full allegiance only to that coming from the Word, which demands we renounce independence and conform selves to the Reality which is Christ.	Reformers (less Luther than Calvin and others) F. D. Maurice Karl Barth	Paul Lehmann
	2 HE IS THE SANCTIFIER	Texts which note how Christ's Spirit changes or transforms the powers of a person who comes under His influence	SANCTIFICATION	REGENERATING PERSON & POWER	Both "old" and "new", sinners and saved, with stress on the effects of the new life in the subjective states of man, blurring the "relational" symbols of the creation-redemption tradition	Be open to the changes that can be worked in us in revivalist conversions and disciplined piety; to cooperate with the sanctifying force of the Spirit, the Word, and the sacraments; to concentrate on the conversion of intention, will and heart.	Thomas Aquinas John Wesley Schleiermacher Bushnell	G. Gilleman, B. Haring, Dietrich Von Hildebrand, Charles Curran

3	HE IS THE JUSTIFIER	JUSTIFICATION	The "have-have not" paradoxical texts, esp. the Pauline texts that show man is both freed and yet in bondage	"END" OF LAW	Both "old" and "new", sinful and just, with the stress on the objectivity of this change; what makes man just is outside him, "declaring" him such, and blurring the subjective changes that embody this	Be free from legalism and self-justifying ethics; confess sinfulness, be converted and walk free, always in need of constant conversion	Luther	R. Bultmann, R. Niebuhr
4	HE IS THE MASTER, MODEL TEACHER	DISCIPLE-SHIP	The texts calling for discipleship, imitation, and the keeping of His commands (including the command of "love")	THE IDEAL MAN	Generally good and capable of striving after perfection, can find peace and happiness in committing themselves to some participation in the life and teachings of Jesus, blurring objective relations and focusing on personal holiness	Follow, imitate, obey, or to learn a lesson from this man, in a variety of Jesus-pieties.	Jefferson and Lincoln, Schleiermacher's Vorbild, Urbild, Soren Kierkegaard, Newman Smyth, 19th c. R. C. Nachfolge school	Joseph Sittler, Charles Sheldon, Carl F. H. Henry, Walter Rauschenbusch, Martin Luther King, Jr.

* Data for this chart comes from Christ and the Moral Life by James M. Gustafson (Harper & Row, Publishers, 1968).

Index

Index